THE COMPREHENSIVE OWNERS HANDBOOK TO CAVALIER KING CHARLES SPANIEL

Mastering The Art Of Owning, Training, and Raising a Joyful and Well-Behaved Dog

Derrick Lucas

COPYRIGHT

DISCLAIMER

The author and publisher have made every effort to ensure the accuracy and completeness of the information contained in this book. However, they assume no responsibility for errors, inaccuracies, omissions, or any other inconsistencies herein. This book is not intended to provide legal, financial, or other professional advice.

TABLE OF CONTENT

CHAPTER 1

Breed History

What is a Cavalier King Charles Spaniel?

The Cavalier King Charles Spaniel is a small but strikingly elegant breed, known for its expressive, soulful eyes, long ears, and soft, flowing coat. Often called "Cavaliers," these dogs fall under the toy group due to their compact size, though their personalities and affectionate nature have them readily fitting into family settings and companionship roles. They're cherished for their friendly demeanor and adaptability, making them ideal for various lifestyles, from city apartments to rural homes.

Their appearance is both distinctive and versatile, with a medium-length coat that can come in four recognized color patterns: Blenheim, Tricolor, Black and Tan, and Ruby. Each coat pattern gives the Cavalier a unique look, allowing owners to choose one that suits their aesthetic preferences. The breed has earned a reputation as a "lap dog" thanks to their innate love for human touch and attention, yet they're surprisingly versatile and can enjoy outdoor activities like moderate hiking or play in a dog park. While they are mild-tempered and gentle, they also have a playful side and enjoy a good run or spirited game, making them well-suited for families with children or other pets.

History of the Cavalier King Charles Spaniel

The history of the Cavalier King Charles Spaniel is deeply intertwined with British nobility, particularly in the 16th and 17th centuries. Originating in the courts of British monarchs, particularly under King Charles I and his son, King Charles II, this breed quickly became a staple of royal life. King Charles II was famously captivated by these small spaniels and often kept them by his side. The breed's association with royalty solidified the spaniels' place as beloved pets of the aristocracy.

The breed initially descended from small spaniels that were popular in European courts, and its predecessors were known as "comfort dogs." These spaniels were often depicted in paintings and tapestries, lounging in the laps of noblewomen or accompanying aristocrats on their travels. They were more than mere companions; it was believed they had a therapeutic effect and could provide warmth and comfort during illnesses or bouts of sadness. This early form of the breed was also valued for its ability to hunt small game, making it a dual-purpose pet and working dog.

The modern Cavalier King Charles Spaniel we know today came about through a deliberate restoration of the original "Toy Spaniel" look, which had shifted over time. By the 18th and 19th centuries, selective breeding practices had introduced shorter noses and rounder skulls, leading to what we now know as the English Toy Spaniel or King Charles Spaniel in Britain. However, in the 1920s, American dog enthusiast Roswell Eldridge offered a reward for breeders who could produce a dog with the original long-nosed, flat-headed appearance seen in portraits of King Charles II. This sparked renewed interest in the "old type" spaniels, ultimately leading to the Cavalier King Charles Spaniel's official recognition as a distinct breed in 1945. Since then, the breed has gained popularity worldwide and continues to win the hearts of dog lovers everywhere.

Physical Characteristics

The Cavalier King Charles Spaniel is a compact, balanced dog that typically weighs between 13 to 18 pounds and stands 12 to 13 inches tall. Their coat is one of their most defining features, soft and silky, often wavy but not overly curly. The ears are long and feathered, framing the dog's expressive face and large, round eyes, which give the breed a characteristic look of warmth and friendliness.

Their four coat colors each contribute to the breed's distinctive appearance. The **Blenheim** color pattern, a rich chestnut and white combination, is perhaps the most recognizable, with a unique "thumbprint" marking on the forehead. The **Tricolor** pattern showcases black and white with tan highlights on the eyebrows, cheeks, and under the tail. The **Black and Tan** Cavaliers have a glossy black coat with rich tan markings, while **Ruby** Cavaliers display a solid, deep red coat.

A notable feature of the Cavalier is its expressive, large, round eyes, which are set apart and add to their gentle and friendly expression. Their tails, often carried cheerfully, show their enthusiastic nature and high spirits. The physical traits of the Cavalier contribute to their natural appeal, which, coupled with their sweet disposition, make them a charming breed.

Typical Breed Behavior

Cavalier King Charles Spaniels are known for their incredibly friendly and affectionate personalities. Their temperament is typically gentle, making them excellent companions for a variety of households, including those with children or elderly family members. Cavaliers are highly social and tend to form strong bonds with their families, often shadowing their human companions around the house. They crave human interaction and can become anxious or depressed if left alone for long periods, making them better suited for owners who have time for daily engagement.

While they are generally easygoing, Cavaliers do have an innate hunting instinct, as they were originally bred from spaniels used in small game hunting. This means they may exhibit a bit of curiosity or chase small animals like squirrels or birds during outdoor activities. However, their hunting drive is typically mild, and with proper training, they can enjoy off-leash activities in secure environments.

The breed is known for its adaptability and ability to adjust to different living conditions. Whether in a bustling city apartment or a spacious country home, Cavaliers thrive as long as they have their family nearby. Their moderate exercise needs mean they enjoy daily walks and playtime but are equally content with lounging at home. Cavaliers are also quick learners and respond well to positive reinforcement, making them relatively easy to train. However, they are sensitive dogs, so harsh training methods can cause them to become anxious or withdrawn.

Is the Cavalier King Charles Spaniel the Right Dog for You?

While the Cavalier King Charles Spaniel's affectionate nature and adaptable personality make them appealing, potential owners should consider whether they can meet the breed's specific needs. Cavaliers thrive on companionship, so they're best suited for individuals or families who can spend quality time with them. These dogs don't do well with long hours alone and can develop separation anxiety if left by themselves frequently. Owners who work from home, are retired, or have flexible schedules often make ideal companions for Cavaliers.

Due to their moderate exercise requirements, Cavaliers are suitable for both active and more sedentary lifestyles, though they do need daily walks and some playtime to maintain their physical health. Their compact size makes them an excellent choice for apartment living, but they are equally happy in homes with yards where they can explore safely. They are also known for their gentle nature with children and can adapt to living with other pets, especially when socialized from a young age.

Health considerations are another important factor. While Cavaliers are generally a robust breed, they are prone to certain genetic health issues, particularly mitral valve disease, which affects the heart, as well as syringomyelia, a neurological condition. Prospective owners should be prepared for regular vet visits and may want to consider pet insurance or a savings plan for potential medical expenses. Reputable breeders will conduct health screenings for common breed issues, so working with a responsible breeder can help mitigate some of these risks.

Cavalier King Charles Spaniels also require regular grooming to keep their coat in good condition. Their long ears and feathered coats are prone to tangling, and they benefit from weekly brushing to prevent mats and keep their fur soft and shiny. In addition, routine ear cleaning is essential, as their floppy ears can be prone to infections.

Ultimately, Cavaliers are a good match for people seeking a loving, low-maintenance companion with a gentle disposition. They are happiest when they feel like a part of the family and can participate in daily activities. For those who can provide a loving home, a Cavalier King Charles Spaniel offers boundless loyalty, affection, and companionship. However, potential owners should be prepared to give them the time, care, and attention they need to thrive. With their royal heritage and endearing personality, Cavaliers remain one of the most beloved companion dogs today.

CHAPTER 2

Choosing Your Cavalier King Charles Spaniel

Buying vs. Adopting

When deciding to bring a Cavalier King Charles Spaniel into your home, one of the first choices to consider is whether to buy from a breeder or adopt from a shelter or rescue organization. Each option has its advantages and disadvantages, depending on your circumstances and goals.

Buying from a breeder allows you to know your puppy's genetic background and often gives you access to detailed health history, including information on parents and lineage. Many people prefer this route when looking for a specific temperament, appearance, or health background. Breeders can provide insight into the dog's family traits, helping you anticipate certain physical or behavioral characteristics that might develop as the puppy grows.

On the other hand, adoption has significant merits and is often seen as a more ethical choice. Animal shelters and rescue organizations offer Cavalier King Charles Spaniels of various ages, often including young puppies and older dogs. Adopting a dog can be rewarding, especially when giving a second chance to a dog in need. Many adoptable Cavaliers may already be house-trained and socialized, which can ease the transition into your home. Additionally, adoption is often less expensive than buying from a breeder and can help reduce the demand for commercial breeding.

The Difference Between Animal Shelters and Rescue Organizations

Understanding the difference between animal shelters and rescue organizations can help you choose the best option for your needs if you decide to adopt.

Animal shelters are often run by municipalities or non-profit organizations and serve as temporary housing for abandoned, stray, or surrendered pets. Shelters typically have a wide range of breeds, ages, and sizes, and most operate on a first-come, first-served basis for adoptions. Dogs in shelters may have limited information on their past, and they may have undergone little training or socialization. However, shelter staff work to provide basic care and behavioral assessments to help you choose a suitable pet.

Rescue organizations, on the other hand, tend to specialize in specific breeds and often work with foster families who provide dogs with a more stable, home-like environment. Breed-specific rescues for Cavalier King Charles Spaniels are available, allowing prospective owners to find a dog that suits their lifestyle. Rescue organizations usually know more about the dog's history, health, and personality, as they spend time observing the dog in a home setting. This can be particularly helpful when adopting a Cavalier, as you can get a better sense of the dog's temperament and how they interact with other pets or children.

Tips for Adopting a Cavalier King Charles Spaniel

Adopting a Cavalier King Charles Spaniel can be a rewarding experience, but it's essential to approach the process thoughtfully to find the right match. Here are some tips to help make your adoption journey successful:

1. **Research the breed**: Cavaliers are affectionate and social dogs that thrive on companionship. Ensure your lifestyle aligns with their needs, including time for regular exercise, grooming, and plenty of human interaction.
2. **Visit local shelters and rescues**: Spend time observing the available dogs to see which ones

show interest in you. Look for body language that indicates friendliness, like wagging tails, soft eyes, and relaxed postures. Some Cavaliers may be shy or nervous, especially if they've had a difficult past, but patience can help them warm up.

3. **Ask questions about the dog's history**: The more you know about the dog's background, the better. Inquire about previous homes, medical history, behavior with other pets, and training levels. This will help you determine if the dog fits well into your household.

4. **Evaluate the dog's temperament**: Rescue organizations often conduct temperament testing, which can be very helpful in identifying behavioral tendencies. For example, a dog with a calm disposition may be well-suited for a family with young children, while a more active or energetic dog might be better for someone with an active lifestyle.

5. **Prepare your home**: Cavaliers are sensitive dogs and will need a peaceful, safe environment to adjust to their new home. Make sure you have basic supplies like a bed, toys, and grooming tools ready.

Importance of Breeder Reputation

If you decide to buy from a breeder, choosing a reputable breeder is essential to ensure the long-term health and well-being of your Cavalier King Charles Spaniel. Unfortunately, irresponsible breeding practices are common in the dog world, and Cavaliers are no exception. Due to their popularity, some breeders prioritize profit over the health and welfare of their dogs, resulting in poorly bred puppies with numerous health problems.

A reputable breeder prioritizes the health, temperament, and overall quality of their puppies. They will conduct thorough health screenings on the breeding dogs, looking for genetic issues common in Cavaliers, such as heart disease and syringomyelia. This level of care requires time and investment, and reputable breeders are usually upfront about the costs and waiting lists associated with acquiring a well-bred Cavalier.

Finding the Right Breeder

Finding the right breeder may take time, but it's worth the effort to ensure your Cavalier is healthy and well-adjusted. Here are some key steps in identifying a responsible breeder:

1. **Research and referrals**: Start by looking for breeders recommended by recognized breed clubs, such as the American Cavalier King

Charles Spaniel Club (ACKCSC). Breed clubs uphold standards and often keep lists of approved breeders who meet specific health and breeding criteria.

2. **Visit the breeder's facility**: Reputable breeders are transparent and welcome visitors. Visiting allows you to see the environment where the puppies are raised, assess the cleanliness, and observe the dogs' interactions with the breeder. If a breeder refuses visits, consider it a red flag.

3. **Ask about health tests**: Cavaliers are prone to certain genetic issues. A good breeder will screen their breeding dogs for conditions like mitral valve disease, hip dysplasia, and eye disorders. Ask to see proof of these health tests.

4. **Meet the puppy's parents**: Meeting the puppy's parents can give you insight into the puppy's potential temperament and appearance. It's also a good opportunity to see if the breeding dogs are healthy and well-cared for.

5. **Check for breeder support**: Many responsible breeders offer lifelong support for their puppies, often providing resources, advice, and guidance for new owners. Some even require that the dog be returned to them if the owner can no longer care for it.

Breeder Contracts and Guarantees

A reputable breeder will usually have a contract outlining the terms of the sale, health guarantees, and conditions for ownership. This contract protects both you and the breeder and ensures that you're receiving a healthy puppy.

Most breeder contracts include a health guarantee, specifying that the puppy is free from serious genetic issues for a certain period. If a health problem arises within the guaranteed time frame, the breeder may offer a partial refund, cover medical costs, or provide a replacement puppy.

It's essential to read the contract thoroughly and clarify any questions you have before signing. Pay close attention to sections about health guarantees, return policies, and expectations of the owner. A good breeder is invested in the puppy's lifelong well-being and will often include terms that require the dog to be returned to them if you can no longer provide care.

Picking the Perfect Puppy

Once you've selected a breeder or rescue organization, the next step is choosing the right puppy. The process can be exciting but overwhelming, as each puppy may have unique characteristics and temperaments. Here are some guidelines for picking the perfect Cavalier King Charles Spaniel puppy:

1. **Observe the litter**: Take time to watch the puppies interact with each other. This can reveal early signs of their personalities. Some puppies may be more adventurous, while others are reserved. Consider what type of personality will best suit your household.
2. **Check for health indicators**: Look for signs of good health, such as bright eyes, clean ears, and a shiny coat. Avoid puppies with runny noses, red eyes, or signs of lethargy, as these could indicate underlying health issues.
3. **Assess the puppy's confidence**: A well-socialized puppy will show curiosity and confidence when interacting with people. A puppy that is overly fearful or aggressive may require more extensive training and socialization.
4. **Get a veterinarian check-up**: Before finalizing your choice, ensure the puppy has been examined by a veterinarian and received initial vaccinations. Reputable breeders will provide vaccination records and a certificate of health for the puppy.

The Different Puppy Personality Types

Understanding different personality types can help you pick a puppy that will best fit your lifestyle. Here are some common puppy personality types you might encounter:

1. **The Leader**: This puppy is confident, assertive, and enjoys taking charge. While they can make wonderful pets, they may require firm training and boundaries, as they tend to push limits.
2. **The Social Butterfly**: Friendly and outgoing, this type loves people and other animals. They are generally easy to train and adjust well to various social settings, making them ideal for families.
3. **The Thinker**: This puppy may be more observant and cautious, carefully assessing new situations before jumping in. Thinkers can be thoughtful and loyal but may require patience and encouragement to build confidence.
4. **The Clown**: Playful and spirited, this type loves to entertain and is always looking for ways to have fun. They tend to be good with children and other pets but may require guidance to manage their energy.
5. **The Gentle Soul**: Sensitive and mild-tempered, this puppy is calm and affectionate, making them a good fit for quieter households. They thrive on gentle interaction and may be more reserved in unfamiliar environments.

Selecting a Cavalier King Charles Spaniel that aligns with your lifestyle and family dynamics ensures a harmonious relationship for years to come. With thoughtful preparation and research, you can bring home a healthy, happy companion that fits perfectly into your life.

CHAPTER 3

Preparing for Your Cavalier King Charles Spaniel

Bringing a Cavalier King Charles Spaniel into your home is an exciting milestone, but preparation is key to ensuring a smooth transition for both your new dog and everyone else in the household. Cavaliers are known for their gentle, friendly nature and thrive in environments where they feel safe, loved, and included. By taking the time to puppy-proof your home, gather the necessary supplies, and prepare children and other pets, you'll set up your new Cavalier for success in their forever home.

Preparing Children and Other Pets

Introducing a new dog to children and existing pets should be handled carefully to establish a positive relationship and avoid any potential conflicts. Cavaliers are generally gentle with children and other animals, but a structured introduction is still essential to prevent misunderstandings and to allow everyone to adapt gradually.

Preparing Children

Teach children to be gentle and respectful with your new Cavalier King Charles Spaniel. Before the dog arrives, explain that dogs have different ways of communicating and that certain behaviors, like hugging tightly or pulling on their ears, can be overwhelming. Show children how to pet the dog gently, preferably on the chest or sides rather than the top of the head, which can feel intimidating to some dogs. Set rules around giving the dog space when they're eating or resting.

Involving children in age-appropriate dog care tasks, like filling the water bowl or helping with gentle brushing, can also foster a sense of responsibility and establish a bond with the dog. Remind them that dogs have different energy levels throughout the day, and sometimes, especially when the dog is new, they need quiet time to acclimate.

Introducing Other Pets

If you have other pets, especially another dog or cat, introduce them to the new Cavalier gradually. Start by allowing them to sniff each other from a safe distance while on leashes, ideally in a neutral area rather than one animal's primary living space. If possible, introduce them outdoors, where both pets may feel less territorial. Keep the initial interactions brief and positive, gradually increasing their time together over several days. Supervise all interactions to ensure that they go smoothly, and don't force them if either animal appears uncomfortable.

For households with cats, give the cat an elevated or separate space where they can observe the new dog from a distance. Many Cavaliers adapt well to cats due to their gentle and friendly nature, but respecting your cat's need for a gradual introduction will help avoid stress. Encourage positive reinforcement with treats for both pets when they behave calmly around each other.

Puppy-Proofing Your Home

Just like a toddler, a curious puppy is likely to get into things they shouldn't. Puppy-proofing your home is essential to create a safe environment where your Cavalier can explore without risk.

1. **Remove hazardous items**: Puppies are prone to chewing anything within reach, so make sure to remove or secure small items, such as buttons, batteries, and children's toys. Electrical cords, plants, and cleaning supplies should also be kept out of reach or blocked off.
2. **Secure trash bins**: The smell of food can be irresistible to a Cavalier puppy, and trash bins often contain items that are dangerous if ingested. Use bins with secure lids or store them in cabinets to prevent any potential incidents.

3. **Block off restricted areas**: Set up baby gates to limit your puppy's access to certain areas of your home, such as staircases, bathrooms, or rooms with delicate furniture. This helps keep them safe while they learn boundaries within the home.
4. **Store medications and cleaning products securely**: Many household products can be toxic to dogs. Ensure that medications, cleaning products, and other chemicals are stored in cabinets that your dog cannot open.
5. **Check furniture stability**: Cavalier puppies are curious and may attempt to jump on furniture, which could lead to accidents if something is unstable. Ensure that bookcases, tables, and decorative items are secure, especially in areas where your puppy will have access.

Dangerous Things Your Dog Might Eat

Cavalier King Charles Spaniels are known to be curious eaters, so it's crucial to be aware of everyday household items that may pose health risks if ingested.

1. **Human foods**: Many foods we enjoy, such as chocolate, grapes, onions, garlic, and caffeine, are toxic to dogs. Keep these foods out of reach and educate family members about which items are unsafe for dogs.

2. **Plants**: Some plants commonly found in homes, like lilies, poinsettias, and philodendrons, are toxic to dogs. Either remove these plants or place them in an area your dog can't access.

3. **Medications**: Even over-the-counter medications like ibuprofen and acetaminophen are dangerous for dogs. Always store medications securely and never leave pills where your dog might find them.

4. **Household chemicals**: Cleaning supplies, insecticides, and certain beauty products can be harmful if ingested. Always store these items out of your dog's reach and avoid using harsh chemicals on surfaces your dog frequently comes in contact with.

5. **Small objects**: Items like buttons, coins, rubber bands, and batteries are easy for a small dog to swallow. Cavalier puppies may be especially prone to picking up small objects with their mouths, so check floors regularly and keep such items out of reach.

Supplies to Purchase Before You Bring Your Cavalier King Charles Spaniel

Being well-prepared with the necessary supplies can make the transition smoother for both you and your Cavalier.

1. **Collar and leash**: A comfortable, adjustable collar and a leash of appropriate length are essential. Choose a lightweight collar to suit the Cavalier's small size and delicate neck.

2. **Identification tag**: Include your phone number and any relevant contact information on your dog's ID tag. Microchipping your dog provides an added layer of security in case they get lost.

3. **Food and water bowls**: Opt for stainless steel or ceramic bowls, as these are easy to clean and less likely to harbor bacteria than plastic ones.

4. **Dog bed**: A soft, comfortable bed will provide your Cavalier with a cozy space to rest. Cavaliers are prone to joint issues as they age, so consider an orthopedic bed to offer additional support.

5. **Crate**: A crate is valuable for training and offers a safe space for your puppy when you're not available to supervise. Make sure the crate is large enough for your dog to stand, turn around, and lie down comfortably.

6. **Toys**: Chew toys, puzzle toys, and soft plush toys can provide mental stimulation and prevent boredom. Ensure toys are appropriately sized for your Cavalier to avoid choking hazards.

7. **Grooming supplies**: Cavaliers require regular grooming to maintain their coat. Stock up on a brush, comb, nail clippers, and dog-friendly

shampoo to keep your dog's coat and nails in good condition.

8. **Training treats**: Small, soft treats are useful for training sessions and positive reinforcement. Choose treats that are easy to chew and not too high in calories.

Preparing an Indoor Space

Your Cavalier King Charles Spaniel will need a comfortable, safe area indoors where they can feel at ease. Designate a space for their bed and food and water bowls, ideally in a quiet, low-traffic area of the house. Ensure that this space is free from drafts, excessive noise, and direct sunlight.

Create a Routine Area

Dogs thrive on routine, so establish consistent areas for feeding, sleeping, and play. Set up your puppy's crate in a central location where they can see the family, as Cavaliers are social dogs and enjoy being around people. Placing the crate in a room where you spend a lot of time will also help your Cavalier feel included in daily activities.

Bathroom Area

For house training, designate a specific area for bathroom breaks and be consistent in taking your puppy to this spot. Consistency will help reinforce positive behaviors, making the training process smoother.

Preparing an Outdoor Space

A secure outdoor area is important for exercise and playtime. Cavaliers enjoy moderate activity and can be quite playful, so a backyard or fenced area will allow them to explore safely.

Fencing

Make sure the outdoor space is securely fenced, as Cavaliers are small dogs and may find ways to escape through small gaps. Ensure that gates close properly, and check the fencing regularly for any weak spots.

Provide Shade and Shelter

Cavaliers have a soft, luxurious coat that can make them sensitive to extreme temperatures. If your dog will be spending time outside, ensure that there is adequate shade and shelter from direct sunlight and rain.

Remove Potential Hazards

Check your yard for potential hazards such as toxic plants, sharp objects, and small items that could be swallowed. Clear any tools or equipment from areas where your dog will play, and avoid using harsh chemicals on your lawn, as they may be harmful if ingested or come into contact with your dog's paws.

CHAPTER 4

Bringing Home Your Cavalier King Charles Spaniel

Bringing home a Cavalier King Charles Spaniel is an exciting and memorable experience that marks the beginning of a long-lasting relationship filled with joy and companionship. However, the process involves careful planning and preparation to ensure that both you and your new dog feel comfortable and settled from the start. This chapter provides a comprehensive guide on how to make your dog's first days and nights with you as smooth and stress-free as possible, from picking up your new pet to managing the first vet visit, and understanding the financial commitments involved in owning a Cavalier.

Picking up Your Cavalier King Charles Spaniel

The day you bring your new Cavalier home is one that you'll likely remember forever. To make it as comfortable as possible for both you and your new pet, there are a few things to consider before picking them up.

1. **Set up a Pick-Up Plan**: Coordinate a time to pick up your Cavalier that allows you to spend the day and night with them without interruptions. Puppies can feel nervous in new environments, so having a calm, relaxed environment waiting for them will help ease the transition.

2. **Bring Essentials**: Bring a comfortable crate or pet carrier for the ride home, as well as a soft blanket that has been in the dog's original home or with the breeder. Familiar scents can provide comfort during this potentially stressful transition. Additionally, bring a collar, leash, and water in case the trip is longer than expected.

3. **Keep It Calm and Quiet**: While it's tempting to invite friends or family to meet the new addition, the first day should be a quiet, calm experience for your Cavalier. Too much stimulation could overwhelm them, leading to stress or fear that may affect their initial adjustment.

The Ride Home

The ride home is your Cavalier's first introduction to their new life, so making it as calm and comfortable as possible is essential. Many dogs experience anxiety during car rides, particularly if it's their first one, so preparing for this journey will help prevent stress for both of you.

1. **Secure the Dog Safely**: Place your dog in a crate or carrier for the ride home. This is the safest option, as it prevents your dog from moving around in the car, reducing the risk of accidents. It also provides a cozy, enclosed space where they can feel secure.

2. **Drive Calmly**: Cavaliers are generally calm by nature, but a bumpy or erratic car ride could unsettle even the most relaxed dog. Drive smoothly, avoid sudden stops, and keep the radio at a low volume to help ease any travel anxiety.

3. **Offer Reassurance**: If your dog is feeling anxious, speak to them in a calm and soothing tone. Avoid sudden loud noises and, if possible, have a family member or friend sit in the back seat next to the crate to provide comfort and reassurance throughout the journey.

4. **Plan for Stops if Necessary**: If you have a long drive ahead, make sure to stop for bathroom breaks. However, be cautious when letting your Cavalier out of the car, as they might be scared and try to bolt. Always keep them on a leash when they're outside.

The First Night

Your Cavalier's first night at home can be challenging for both of you, as they adjust to a completely new environment and you establish new routines. Preparing in advance for this first night will help create a comforting experience that sets the tone for their future behavior in the home.

1. **Create a Cozy Sleeping Space**: Choose a quiet, low-traffic area for your dog's sleeping space. A soft dog bed placed inside their crate or in a designated corner of the room will provide them with a secure, cozy spot. Adding a familiar-scented blanket from their previous home can provide additional comfort.

2. **Set Up a Nighttime Routine**: Establish a consistent nighttime routine from the very beginning. For example, take your Cavalier out for a final bathroom break, give them a few minutes of calm petting or playtime, and then lead them to their sleeping area. Routines help dogs feel secure and can reduce anxiety.

3. **Expect Some Whining**: Cavaliers, especially puppies, may whine or cry during the first few nights as they adjust to sleeping alone. Resist the temptation to pick them up or take them out of the crate when they whine, as this may reinforce the behavior. Instead, reassure them with a calm

voice or gentle patting, and give them time to settle down on their own.

4. **Limit Bathroom Breaks**: Puppies, in particular, have small bladders and may need to go out once or twice during the night. However, keep these bathroom breaks low-key. Take them outside, allow them to go to the bathroom, and then guide them calmly back to bed without engaging in playtime or interaction.

The First Vet Visit

The first veterinary visit is a critical step in your dog's transition, setting a foundation for their health and well-being. Ideally, schedule the appointment within the first few days of bringing your Cavalier home to ensure they're healthy and up to date on necessary vaccinations and treatments.

1. **Choose a Veterinarian**: If you haven't already selected a vet, now is the time to do so. Look for a veterinarian experienced with small dog breeds like Cavaliers, as they can have unique health considerations, such as heart issues, that may require specific care.

2. **Bring Necessary Documents**: Bring any medical records, vaccination history, and paperwork from the breeder or shelter. This information helps the

vet create a comprehensive health profile for your Cavalier.

3. **Discuss Breed-Specific Health Concerns**: Cavaliers are prone to specific health issues, including heart disease (mitral valve disease), hip dysplasia, and eye problems. Talk to the vet about these concerns and ask about preventive measures or early screenings that can help you monitor your dog's health over time.

4. **Start a Vaccination and Treatment Schedule**: Your vet will discuss a vaccination schedule tailored to your dog's age and lifestyle. They will also guide you on preventive care, such as flea, tick, and heartworm prevention, as well as the ideal timing for spaying or neutering, if applicable.

5. **Ask Questions**: Don't hesitate to ask any questions you may have about caring for your Cavalier. Whether it's about diet, exercise, grooming, or behavior, your veterinarian is there to support you and help ensure that your dog's transition is as smooth as possible.

The Cost of Ownership

Understanding the financial commitment involved in owning a Cavalier King Charles Spaniel is essential, as the costs can extend beyond the initial purchase or adoption fee. Being prepared for ongoing expenses will ensure you're fully equipped to provide the best care for your dog throughout their life.

1. **Initial Costs**: The initial costs of bringing home a Cavalier can include adoption or purchase fees, initial vet visits, vaccinations, and necessary supplies like crates, beds, collars, and leashes. These initial expenses can range from a few hundred to several thousand dollars, depending on whether you adopt or buy from a breeder.

2. **Routine Veterinary Care**: Cavaliers, like all dogs, require regular veterinary visits for vaccinations, dental cleanings, and health screenings. Routine care may cost anywhere from $200 to $500 annually, depending on the specific care your dog requires.

3. **Health Insurance**: Due to their predisposition to certain health conditions, investing in pet health insurance is a smart choice for Cavalier owners. Monthly premiums vary, with comprehensive plans ranging from $30 to $60 per month. Insurance can help offset the cost of unexpected medical treatments, which may otherwise be costly.

4. **Food and Treats**: High-quality dog food and treats are essential for your Cavalier's health and well-being. Expect to spend around $30 to $50

per month on food, with treats adding an extra $5 to $15. Opt for food formulated for small breeds with ingredients that support joint, heart, and coat health.

5. **Grooming and Supplies**: Cavaliers require regular grooming, including brushing, nail trimming, and occasional professional grooming. Professional grooming costs can range from $30 to $60 per session, and it's recommended to have your dog groomed every few months. Grooming tools, such as brushes, combs, and nail clippers, will also add to the cost.

6. **Training**: If you choose to invest in obedience classes or training sessions, these can cost between $100 and $300, depending on the duration and quality of the program. While Cavaliers are generally well-behaved, early training can be beneficial for establishing good habits.

7. **Emergency Costs**: Unexpected medical costs can arise, and Cavaliers are prone to certain health conditions. Setting aside an emergency fund of at least a few hundred dollars is advisable to cover any unforeseen expenses that insurance may not fully cover.

CHAPTER 5

Being a Puppy Parent

Becoming a Cavalier King Charles Spaniel puppy parent is a joyful journey, but it's also filled with challenges and responsibilities. Raising a puppy requires patience, understanding, and commitment as you guide your new companion through the first critical stages of life. This chapter offers practical tips and insights into managing your puppy's behavior, setting expectations, and establishing routines that will help them grow into a well-behaved, confident adult dog. From dealing with common behavioral issues to mastering crate training and managing separation anxiety, you'll find everything you need to ensure that your Cavalier thrives under your care.

Have Realistic Expectations

Bringing home a Cavalier King Charles Spaniel puppy can be a lot of fun, but it's important to set realistic expectations. Puppies are energetic, curious, and sometimes mischievous, and their behavior may take time to shape into the well-mannered companion you envision. Here are a few things to keep in mind:

1. **Patience is Key**: Cavaliers are generally eager to please, but training doesn't happen overnight. Consistency and repetition will be essential as they learn acceptable behaviors, and they may need gentle reminders along the way.
2. **Puppy Energy is Normal**: Cavaliers are playful, social, and spirited, especially as puppies. Expect bursts of energy throughout the day and take advantage of these moments by engaging them in play, short training sessions, or exercise to help them release energy productively.
3. **Accidents Will Happen**: Potty training takes time, and accidents are inevitable. While it can be frustrating, remember that this is a normal part of puppyhood, and your Cavalier will improve with consistent guidance.
4. **Bonding Takes Time**: Building a deep bond with your puppy is a gradual process. Through daily care, affection, and consistent routines, your Cavalier will develop a strong sense of trust and attachment.

Chewing

Chewing is a natural and necessary behavior for puppies, helping them relieve teething discomfort and explore their environment. However, this instinct can sometimes lead to destructive behavior if not properly managed.

1. **Provide Appropriate Chew Toys**: Offer a variety of chew toys to keep your Cavalier entertained and to prevent them from turning to furniture, shoes, or other household items. Look for toys that are safe, durable, and designed specifically for small breeds.

2. **Redirect Chewing**: If you catch your puppy chewing on an inappropriate item, calmly redirect them to a toy. Avoid scolding or punishing, as this may confuse your puppy and make them anxious. Instead, praise them when they chew on their toys.

3. **Encourage Positive Chewing Habits**: Reward your Cavalier with praise or treats whenever they use their chew toys. This positive reinforcement helps establish a habit of appropriate chewing.

4. **Puppy-Proof Your Home**: Remove tempting objects from your puppy's reach. Shoes, electrical cords, and other chewable items should be kept out of sight to minimize the risk of accidents or injuries.

Digging

Digging is another instinctive behavior that some Cavaliers may engage in, especially if they're feeling bored, anxious, or in need of physical stimulation.

1. **Provide Mental Stimulation**: Cavaliers are intelligent dogs and can become bored if they don't receive enough mental and physical stimulation. Incorporate interactive play, training sessions, and puzzle toys to keep their minds engaged.

2. **Create a Designated Digging Area**: If digging is a persistent issue and you have a backyard, consider designating a specific area where your puppy is allowed to dig. Encourage them to use this area by burying toys or treats to make it a fun experience.

3. **Address Anxiety and Stress**: Some dogs dig as a way to relieve anxiety or stress. Ensure your puppy is getting enough attention, exercise, and enrichment. If digging is accompanied by other signs of anxiety, such as whining or pacing, consult a veterinarian or professional trainer for guidance.

4. **Discourage Unwanted Digging**: Gently redirect your puppy when you catch them digging in inappropriate areas. Try to provide an alternative activity, such as a toy or a game, to distract them from the digging habit.

Barking and Growling

Barking and growling are normal ways for dogs to communicate, but excessive barking can become a problem if not properly managed.

1. **Understand the Cause**: Cavaliers may bark for various reasons, such as excitement, boredom, fear, or as a response to unfamiliar sounds or people. Observe when and why your puppy barks to better understand the behavior.
2. **Teach the "Quiet" Command**: Teaching your puppy a "quiet" command can be helpful in managing excessive barking. Start by letting them bark a few times, then say "quiet" in a calm, firm voice, and reward them when they stop barking.
3. **Avoid Reinforcing Barking**: If your puppy is barking for attention, avoid reinforcing the behavior by responding to them immediately. Wait until they're quiet before giving attention or treats to encourage calm behavior.
4. **Provide Positive Outlets**: Sometimes, barking is a result of pent-up energy or frustration. Ensure that your Cavalier is getting adequate exercise and playtime to help reduce unwanted vocalizations.

Heel Nipping

Heel nipping is a common issue, especially with herding breeds, but some Cavaliers may display this behavior as puppies, particularly during play.

1. **Redirect the Behavior**: If your puppy nips at your heels, immediately redirect their attention to an appropriate toy. This will help them understand that toys are for biting, not people.
2. **Use Positive Reinforcement**: Reward your puppy with treats or praise when they play gently without nipping. Consistently reinforcing this behavior will help them learn appropriate play etiquette.
3. **Avoid Rough Play**: Rough play can encourage nipping and biting behaviors. Engage in gentle play and avoid games that involve your puppy biting at your hands or feet.
4. **Teach a "No" or "Leave It" Command**: Teaching commands like "no" or "leave it" can be effective for discouraging unwanted behaviors like nipping. Be consistent in using these commands whenever your puppy tries to nip at your heels.

Separation Anxiety

Cavaliers are known for their affectionate and loyal nature, which can make them prone to separation anxiety if left alone for long periods. Addressing this issue early on will help prevent anxiety-related behaviors from developing.

1. **Start with Short Absences**: Begin by leaving your puppy alone for short periods, gradually increasing the duration. This helps them become comfortable with being alone without experiencing stress.
2. **Create a Calm Environment**: When you leave, make sure your puppy's environment is calm and safe. A comfortable crate or playpen, along with familiar toys and blankets, can provide reassurance in your absence.
3. **Avoid Long Goodbyes**: Lengthy goodbyes can signal to your puppy that something is wrong, increasing their anxiety. Keep departures low-key, and avoid fussing over your dog before you leave.
4. **Provide Mental Stimulation**: Interactive toys, such as puzzle feeders, can help keep your puppy occupied and distract them from your absence. These toys engage their mind and can reduce feelings of loneliness.
5. **Consider Professional Help if Needed**: If separation anxiety persists or worsens, consider consulting a professional trainer or behaviorist who can provide specialized guidance.

Crate Training Basics

Crate training can be a valuable tool for managing your puppy's behavior, providing them with a safe space, and aiding in house training. When done correctly, crate training can help your Cavalier feel secure and reduce anxiety.

1. **Make the Crate Inviting**: Start by making the crate a comfortable, positive space for your puppy. Add a soft bed, blankets, and a toy to create a cozy retreat.
2. **Introduce the Crate Gradually**: Allow your puppy to explore the crate at their own pace. Start by leaving the door open and encouraging them to enter with treats or toys. Gradually increase the time they spend inside with the door closed.
3. **Avoid Using the Crate as Punishment**: The crate should be a safe, positive space, so never use it as a form of punishment. This could lead to fear or anxiety associated with the crate.
4. **Establish a Crate Routine**: Use the crate during mealtimes, naps, and bedtime to help establish a routine. This will help your puppy learn that the crate is a normal part of their daily life.
5. **Practice Patience**: Crate training takes time and consistency. Some puppies may adjust quickly, while others may need more time to feel

comfortable. Be patient and encourage positive associations with the crate.

Leaving Your Dog Home Alone

As your puppy grows, they'll need to learn how to spend time alone without feeling anxious or bored. This is essential for their independence and your peace of mind.

1. **Establish a Consistent Routine**: Dogs thrive on routine, so establish a schedule for feeding, play, and alone time. A predictable routine will help your Cavalier feel secure, even when you're not around.
2. **Exercise Before You Leave**: A tired puppy is more likely to relax while you're away. Make sure your Cavalier gets some exercise or playtime before leaving to burn off energy.
3. **Use a Playpen or Crate**: Confining your puppy to a safe area, like a crate or playpen, prevents accidents and destructive behavior. Ensure they have toys and water to keep them occupied while you're away.
4. **Gradual Departure Training**: Start by leaving your puppy alone for just a few minutes, gradually extending the time. This helps them become comfortable with your absence and reduces anxiety.

5. **Provide Enrichment Toys**: Toys that dispense treats or require problem-solving can help keep your puppy engaged and distracted. These toys are particularly useful for solo time, as they provide mental stimulation.

Being a puppy parent to a Cavalier King Charles Spaniel involves patience, love, and consistent guidance. By setting realistic expectations and addressing behavioral issues with positive reinforcement, you'll raise a confident, well-behaved dog who's a joy to have in your home. With the right approach, you'll build a strong, lasting bond with your puppy, ensuring they grow into a happy, loyal companion.

CHAPTER 6

Potty Training Your Cavalier King Charles Spaniel

Potty training is one of the first—and most important—steps in bringing home a Cavalier King Charles Spaniel. While this breed is generally intelligent and eager to please, potty training can still be a challenge, as it is with most puppies. Establishing good habits early on can make life much easier for both you and your dog. In this chapter, we will explore the most effective methods of potty training, provide tips for using a crate, and discuss how to handle accidents. Additionally, we will cover the pros and cons of doggy doors and other techniques for managing your Cavalier's bathroom habits.

Methods of Potty Training

There are several methods of potty training, but the key to success is consistency and patience. Every dog is different, and some methods may work better than others depending on your puppy's personality, your living environment, and your lifestyle. The following methods are the most commonly used for potty training:

1. **Potty Pad Training**: This method is particularly useful for those who live in apartments or have limited outdoor space. Potty pads are absorbent mats that your puppy can use when they need to relieve themselves. They are ideal for apartment dwellers who cannot always take their dog outside quickly. To use potty pads effectively:
   - Place the pad in a designated spot that is easily accessible to your puppy.
   - Encourage your puppy to use the pad by gently guiding them to it after meals, naps, and play sessions.
   - Praise and reward them when they use the pad correctly.
   - Gradually move the pad closer to the door to transition them to using the outdoors when they are older.

2. **Outdoor Potty Training**: This is the most common method for potty training a Cavalier King Charles Spaniel, especially if you have a yard or live in a house with access to outdoor spaces. The process involves taking your puppy outside at regular intervals and rewarding them when they do their business. To get started:

o Take your puppy outside immediately after waking up, after meals, and after playtime. These are the times they are most likely to need to relieve themselves.
o Use a command like "go potty" consistently when you bring them outside to help them associate the phrase with the act of relieving themselves.
o Once your puppy goes potty outside, reward them with praise and a small treat. Positive reinforcement helps them understand that going outside is the correct behavior.
o Be patient, as it may take a few weeks for your puppy to fully understand the process. In the meantime, keep them on a regular schedule to prevent accidents.

3. **Bell Training**: Bell training is a method where your puppy learns to ring a bell to let you know when they need to go outside. This technique is helpful if you want your Cavalier to signal their need to go out, which can reduce accidents in the house.
o Start by hanging a bell on the door you use to take your dog outside.
o Each time you take your puppy out, gently tap the bell with their paw or nose before opening the door. You can also

encourage them to interact with the bell by placing a treat behind it.

○ Over time, your puppy will learn to associate the bell with going outside, and they may begin ringing it on their own when they need to go.

4. **Crate Training for Potty Training**: Crate training can be a very effective potty training method because dogs naturally avoid soiling their sleeping area. By confining your puppy to a crate when you're not able to supervise them, you can help prevent accidents in the house. However, it's important not to leave your puppy in the crate for too long, as this can cause stress or harm to their health. Here's how crate training works:

○ Select a crate that is large enough for your puppy to stand up, turn around, and lie down comfortably but not too large. If the crate is too big, your puppy may be able to use one corner as a bathroom area, defeating the purpose of the training.

○ Start by placing your puppy in the crate for short periods and taking them outside immediately after they are let out.

○ Be sure to take your puppy outside every few hours, especially after eating, drinking, or playing. Use a consistent phrase like "go potty" to help your puppy associate the cue with the action.

5. **Scheduled Potty Breaks**: No matter which method you choose, it's important to establish a consistent potty routine for your puppy. Take them outside or to their potty pad at regular intervals throughout the day—generally every two to three hours, as puppies have small bladders. Additionally, you should take your puppy outside after meals, naps, and playtime, as these are all times when your puppy is most likely to need to go potty.

Using the Crate for Potty Training

The crate can be a valuable tool for potty training, as dogs naturally avoid soiling their sleeping area. By using the crate in combination with a regular schedule of potty breaks, you can help your Cavalier learn when and where it's appropriate to relieve themselves.

1. **Choose the Right Size Crate**: Make sure the crate is large enough for your puppy to stand, lie down, and turn around comfortably but not so large that they can create a bathroom area in one corner. If the crate is too big, consider using a crate divider to adjust the size as your puppy grows.

2. **Use the Crate Sparingly**: Don't leave your puppy in the crate for long periods, especially at the beginning of the potty training process. Puppies, especially young ones, need to relieve themselves regularly. A good rule of thumb is to limit crate time to a few hours at a time, gradually increasing the duration as your puppy matures.

3. **Create a Routine**: Take your puppy outside immediately after letting them out of the crate. This helps to reinforce the idea that they should go potty outside, not inside the crate. Keep your puppy on a schedule and take them outside frequently to reduce the chances of accidents.

4. **Reward Success**: When your puppy successfully goes potty outside after being in the crate, offer them praise and a treat. Positive reinforcement encourages them to repeat the behavior in the future.

The First Few Weeks

The first few weeks of potty training your Cavalier King Charles Spaniel are crucial for setting up a foundation of good habits. Here are some steps to follow during this time:

1. **Establish a Routine**: Consistency is key during the early weeks. Take your puppy outside at

regular intervals and after every meal, nap, and play session. By sticking to a schedule, your puppy will begin to learn when and where it's time to go potty.

2. **Be Patient and Positive**: Potty training can take time, especially for puppies with smaller bladders like Cavaliers. If you have accidents, clean them up immediately using an enzymatic cleaner to remove any scent markers that could encourage future accidents.

3. **Supervise Indoors**: If you're not using a crate, supervise your puppy closely when they're indoors. Watch for signs that they need to go, such as sniffing or circling. If you catch them in the act of having an accident, quickly but calmly take them outside to finish.

4. **Keep Sessions Short and Positive**: Don't make potty training sessions feel like a punishment. If your puppy doesn't go potty right away, don't scold them. Simply bring them back inside and try again after a short break.

How to Handle Accidents

Accidents will happen, especially during the early stages of potty training. It's important to handle accidents in a calm, consistent way so that your puppy doesn't become confused or anxious.

1. **Don't Punish Your Puppy**: Never punish your Cavalier for accidents. Punishment can lead to fear and confusion, which can make potty training even harder. Instead, clean up the mess thoroughly and focus on reinforcing positive behavior.

2. **Use Enzymatic Cleaner**: Always clean up accidents immediately using an enzymatic cleaner. This type of cleaner breaks down the proteins in urine and feces, removing the odor completely so your puppy won't be attracted to the same spot again.

3. **Learn from Mistakes**: If accidents are happening frequently, take a look at your schedule and make adjustments. Is your puppy being taken outside often enough? Are they getting enough exercise or playtime? The more you can adjust to your puppy's needs, the fewer accidents you will have.

Pros and Cons of Doggy Doors

Doggy doors can be a great tool for potty training, especially if you have a yard or outdoor space. They allow your puppy to go outside when they need to relieve themselves, without requiring you to be present each time. However, there are both pros and cons to using a doggy door for potty training your Cavalier.

Pros:

- **Convenience**: Doggy doors provide easy access to the outdoors, allowing your puppy to relieve themselves whenever they need to. This can be especially helpful during potty training when you need to take your puppy outside frequently.
- **Independence**: Using a doggy door can help your puppy develop independence, as they can go out without waiting for you to open the door.
- **Convenience for Busy Owners**: If you have a busy schedule, a doggy door can provide your puppy with the freedom to go outside while you're away.

Cons:

- **Security Concerns**: If you live in an area where security is a concern, a doggy door may allow intruders or other animals into your home.
- **Training Issues**: Some puppies may not understand how to use a doggy door right away, and it may take time to teach them.
- **Weather Conditions**: Depending on the weather, a doggy door may allow cold air, rain, or snow into your home, which can be uncomfortable for both you and your puppy.

Potty training your Cavalier King Charles Spaniel requires patience, consistency, and positive reinforcement. Whether you choose potty pad training, outdoor training, or crate training, the key is to establish a routine and reward success. By handling accidents calmly and using the right tools—like crates or doggy doors—you can ensure that your puppy becomes well-trained and comfortable with their bathroom habits. With the right approach, potty training can be a smooth and successful process, helping you build a strong foundation for a happy, well-behaved dog.

CHAPTER 7

Socializing Your Cavalier King Charles Spaniel

Socialization is one of the most important aspects of raising a well-rounded, confident, and happy Cavalier King Charles Spaniel. A well-socialized dog is typically more adaptable, less anxious, and better able to handle new situations, people, and other animals. This chapter will explore the significance of socialization, how to socialize your Cavalier King Charles Spaniel with other dogs and pets, strategies for socializing adult dogs, and the proper ways to introduce them to new people, especially children. By understanding the process of socialization and the benefits it brings, you'll be able to ensure that your Cavalier grows up to be a well-behaved, friendly companion.

Importance of Socialization

Socialization refers to the process of exposing your dog to various people, environments, sounds, and experiences in a positive way, so they learn to handle the world around them confidently. It is essential for a

Cavalier King Charles Spaniel's development and well-being, as improper or insufficient socialization can lead to behavior problems, fear, anxiety, and aggression. Puppies are most impressionable between the ages of 3 and 14 weeks, but it's never too late to begin socializing your dog, even as an adult.

Cavalier King Charles Spaniels are generally friendly, affectionate, and well-mannered dogs. They are known for being particularly sociable with humans, but they can sometimes become shy or nervous around unfamiliar situations or animals. Proper socialization can help curb these behaviors and set them up for success.

The benefits of early and consistent socialization include:

1. **Improved Confidence**: Socializing your Cavalier with new people, places, and situations helps them develop confidence. A well-socialized dog is more likely to approach new experiences without fear or hesitation.
2. **Reduced Fear and Anxiety**: Cavalier King Charles Spaniels, like many small breeds, can be prone to anxiety, especially when faced with unfamiliar environments or loud noises. Socialization helps reduce fear and teaches your dog how to cope with unfamiliar situations.

3. **Better Behavior**: Dogs that are exposed to various stimuli and experiences during their formative months are typically easier to train and less likely to develop undesirable behaviors such as aggression or excessive barking.
4. **Stronger Bond with Owners**: Socializing your dog with people and other animals strengthens your bond. As your dog experiences the world with you, they learn to trust and rely on you for guidance and support.

Behavior Around Other Dogs

Cavalier King Charles Spaniels are typically friendly and tolerant with other dogs, but not all dogs are the same. Early socialization with other dogs helps your Cavalier develop proper canine communication skills, including how to interact respectfully with other dogs and how to read body language.

When socializing your Cavalier with other dogs, it is important to follow these guidelines:

1. **Start with Calm, Friendly Dogs**: If possible, begin socializing your puppy with calm, friendly dogs who are known to be well-behaved. Older dogs who have good manners can teach your Cavalier important lessons about social behavior.

2. **Positive Reinforcement**: Reward your Cavalier for good behavior during dog interactions, such as sitting calmly, sniffing politely, or playing gently. Using treats and praise helps reinforce the desired behaviors.
3. **Supervised Playdates**: Arrange controlled playdates in neutral locations, like a park or a training facility. Always supervise your Cavalier's interactions with other dogs to ensure that play remains friendly and non-aggressive.
4. **Watch for Signs of Stress**: Not all dogs are immediately comfortable with others. If you notice signs of stress, such as growling, snapping, or hiding, it's important to intervene calmly and remove your dog from the situation. Gradually reintroduce them to new dogs in less intense settings if necessary.
5. **Group Classes or Playgroups**: Enrolling your Cavalier in a puppy socialization class or a supervised playgroup is a great way to help them interact with other dogs in a structured, safe environment. These settings provide professional guidance and opportunities for your dog to learn appropriate social skills.

Safe Ways to Socialize with Other Pets

If you have other pets at home, it's essential to properly introduce them to your Cavalier King Charles Spaniel. These introductions should be done in a controlled and gradual manner to ensure that all animals feel comfortable and safe.

1. **Introducing Cats**: If you have a cat, introduce your Cavalier to them slowly. Start by allowing them to sniff each other under a door or through a baby gate. Then, set up controlled face-to-face introductions while keeping both animals on a leash. Never force the interaction. Watch for signs of anxiety or aggression from either animal, and always provide a safe space for each to retreat if they feel overwhelmed.

2. **Introduction to Smaller Pets (Rabbits, Guinea Pigs, etc.)**: When introducing your Cavalier to smaller pets, such as rabbits or guinea pigs, it is important to closely supervise the interaction, as the Cavalier's prey drive could cause them to chase these animals. Start by allowing them to observe the smaller pet from a distance before bringing them closer. Positive reinforcement is key to ensuring your Cavalier behaves calmly and respectfully.

3. **Establishing Boundaries**: Once the initial introduction is made, work on setting boundaries between your Cavalier and other pets. For

example, designate separate sleeping or feeding areas to prevent conflicts. Make sure your dog understands that other pets are part of the family and should be treated with respect.

4. **Reward Calm Behavior**: Whenever your Cavalier behaves calmly around other pets, reward them with praise or treats. This reinforces the idea that peaceful interaction is desirable and helps prevent aggression or anxiety from developing.

Socializing Adult Dogs

While socializing a puppy is often easier, it's important to know that adult Cavalier King Charles Spaniels can still benefit from socialization. Whether you've adopted an older dog or your puppy is now an adult, socialization should continue throughout their life.

1. **Start Slowly**: Adult dogs may be more set in their ways, so it's crucial to take things slowly when socializing them. Gradually introduce new people, animals, and environments to avoid overwhelming them.

2. **Positive Reinforcement**: As with puppies, adult dogs respond well to positive reinforcement. Praise and treat your dog for calm behavior in new situations or with new people. This helps

them associate positive experiences with unfamiliar situations.

3. **Use a Leash for Control**: When socializing an adult dog with new dogs or people, always use a leash to maintain control. This allows you to step in if the situation becomes too overwhelming and helps prevent unwanted interactions.

4. **Desensitization**: If your adult Cavalier has developed fears or anxieties about certain situations (e.g., being around other dogs or going to the vet), desensitization can help. Gradually expose your dog to these situations in a controlled manner, rewarding calm behavior and slowly increasing the level of exposure as your dog becomes more comfortable.

5. **Ongoing Socialization**: Socialization should continue throughout your dog's life, not just in puppyhood. Regular exposure to new experiences, environments, and people helps your Cavalier stay well-adjusted and reduces the chances of anxiety or fear-based behavior.

Greeting New People

Cavalier King Charles Spaniels are generally friendly and affectionate dogs, but it's still important to teach them how to greet new people properly. Without proper guidance, your dog might become overly excitable, jump up on strangers, or be timid in unfamiliar situations.

1. **Teach Proper Greeting Etiquette**: Train your dog to greet new people calmly and politely. Ask visitors to ignore your dog until they have settled down. When your Cavalier is calm, allow them to approach the person and offer a gentle greeting. Reinforce calm behavior with praise and treats.

2. **Socialize with a Variety of People**: Make sure your Cavalier is exposed to different types of people—adults, children, men, women, people with glasses or hats, etc. The more diverse their exposure, the more comfortable they will be with people in general.

3. **Manage Overexcitement**: If your Cavalier tends to get overly excited when greeting new people, practice controlled introductions. Use a leash to maintain control and encourage calm behavior. Reward your dog for sitting or remaining calm rather than jumping or barking.

4. **Teaching Boundaries**: It's important to teach your Cavalier not to jump on new people. Use a consistent "sit" or "stay" command when introducing them to visitors. This not only helps them stay calm but also teaches them proper manners when meeting new people.

Cavalier King Charles Spaniel and Children

Cavalier King Charles Spaniels are generally known for being great with children. Their gentle, affectionate nature makes them excellent companions for kids. However, proper socialization is crucial to ensuring your dog is comfortable around children and knows how to behave.

1. **Introduce Them to Children Gradually**: When introducing your Cavalier to children, start by allowing the dog to approach the child slowly and calmly. Teach children to approach the dog gently and to respect the dog's space, especially during meals or naps.
2. **Supervise Interactions**: Always supervise interactions between young children and your dog. Even the most gentle dogs can become overwhelmed by rough handling, loud noises, or sudden movements. Teach children how to interact respectfully with the dog, such as avoiding pulling on the dog's ears or tail.
3. **Teach Children Dog Etiquette**: Educate children about proper dog etiquette, such as not disturbing the dog when it's eating or resting, not hugging the dog too tightly, and not forcing interactions. This ensures that both the dog and the child feel safe and respected.

4. **Encourage Positive Interactions**: Reward both the dog and the children for positive interactions, such as petting gently, playing calmly, or taking walks together. These experiences help build a positive relationship between your Cavalier and children.

Socializing your Cavalier King Charles Spaniel is essential for their overall development, emotional well-being, and behavior. By introducing them to a variety of people, other dogs, and different environments in a positive, controlled manner, you'll help them become a well-adjusted, confident, and friendly companion. Whether socializing with other dogs, introducing them to children, or helping them get comfortable with new experiences, patience, consistency, and positive reinforcement are key. With the right approach, your Cavalier will grow into a dog who is not only a joy to have at home but also a confident, social member of the community.

CHAPTER 8

Cavalier King Charles Spaniel and Your Other Pets

Owning multiple pets can be a highly rewarding experience, but it requires careful management, patience, and attention to ensure that all animals get along peacefully. The Cavalier King Charles Spaniel, with its friendly and sociable nature, typically integrates well into homes with other pets, including dogs, cats, and even smaller animals like rabbits or guinea pigs. However, as with any breed, there are strategies you need to follow to ensure smooth interspecies relationships. In this chapter, we will explore the process of introducing your Cavalier King Charles Spaniel to other pets, address potential behavioral issues, and provide guidance on managing multiple pets in the same household.

Interspecies Introductions

Introducing your Cavalier King Charles Spaniel to other pets in your home is a gradual process that requires patience and positive reinforcement. While Cavaliers are known for their friendly nature, each pet has its own personality, and their reactions to newcomers will differ. The goal is to make the transition as smooth as possible and avoid any incidents of aggression or fear. Here are some essential steps for successful interspecies introductions:

1. **Start Slow and Safe**: When introducing a new pet to your Cavalier, start by allowing them to meet in neutral territory. For example, if you're introducing your dog to a new cat, allow them to meet through a baby gate or a door before any physical interaction occurs. This prevents your Cavalier from feeling overwhelmed and gives both pets time to adjust to each other's scent and presence without the risk of direct confrontation.

2. **Positive Reinforcement**: Reward both pets with praise, treats, or affection for calm and respectful behavior during the introduction. This helps them associate the new pet with positive experiences and reinforces desirable behavior, like sitting calmly or sniffing politely.

3. **Supervised Interaction**: Always supervise the first few encounters between your Cavalier and any new pet. While Cavaliers are generally gentle and non-aggressive, other pets might not be as accepting. Monitor their body language carefully. If either pet seems stressed or agitated, separate

them and give them time to calm down before trying again. Never force the interaction; let it evolve at its own pace.

4. **Establish Boundaries**: Be clear with your Cavalier and the other pets about boundaries in the home. Make sure each pet has its own designated space, such as a bed or crate, where it can retreat when it needs some alone time. This gives each pet the security of knowing they have a space to call their own, reducing potential conflicts.

5. **Managing Prey Drive**: While Cavaliers are typically friendly and non-aggressive, some may have a mild prey drive, especially around smaller animals like rabbits, guinea pigs, or hamsters. Introduce these pets to your Cavalier with extra caution. Make sure the smaller pets are safe and secure in their enclosures, and never leave them unsupervised with your dog. With proper training and gradual exposure, your Cavalier can learn to coexist peacefully with smaller pets.

6. **Frequent Interactions**: Successful interspecies relationships require consistency. Regular interactions—whether supervised playtime, shared walks, or eating in the same room—help your Cavalier get used to living alongside other pets. Over time, the presence of other animals will become a normal part of their life.

Introducing an Older Cavalier King Charles Spaniel

If you're adding an older Cavalier King Charles Spaniel to your home, the introduction process may require a bit more patience. Adult dogs may have established behaviors, preferences, and territorial instincts that can complicate integration into a new household. Here's how to make the transition smoother:

1. **Consider Their Personality**: Older Cavaliers are usually calm and adaptable, but some may have had negative experiences with other animals or may be less tolerant of change. Before introducing them to other pets, get to know your new dog's temperament and their comfort level with other animals.

2. **Introduction in a Calm Setting**: Much like introducing a puppy, it's important to introduce an older Cavalier in a neutral and calm environment. If you already have pets, ensure that your older Cavalier doesn't feel overwhelmed by too many new stimuli at once. Begin with brief, calm introductions in a controlled space.

3. **Gradual and Controlled Introductions**: Older dogs may need more time to adjust to new pets in the household. Let the introduction happen in

small steps. For example, allow them to sniff each other through a closed door before allowing them to meet face to face. In some cases, it's best to introduce them while they are on a leash so you can control the interaction and ensure no aggressive behaviors occur.

4. **Ensure Routine and Structure**: Older dogs thrive on routine and structure. Maintain a consistent schedule for feeding, exercise, and downtime to help your Cavalier feel secure. Ensure that the introduction doesn't disrupt their daily routine too much, as this can cause unnecessary stress.

5. **Address Existing Behaviors**: If your older Cavalier has been exposed to other pets in the past, they may have learned certain behaviors, whether positive or negative. For instance, they may have been fearful of other dogs or dominant toward cats. Be prepared to address any behavioral challenges that arise, such as redirecting unwanted behaviors, using positive reinforcement, and seeking professional help if needed.

Aggression/Bad Behavior

Though the Cavalier King Charles Spaniel is generally known for being friendly and sociable, no dog is immune to developing behavioral problems. Aggression, territorial behaviors, or bad habits can arise for a variety of reasons, such as poor early socialization, trauma, or stress. Recognizing and addressing these issues early on is essential to ensuring a harmonious home environment for all your pets.

1. **Identify the Cause**: Aggressive or bad behaviors often stem from fear, anxiety, or lack of socialization. Observe your Cavalier's body language to understand why they may be acting out. For example, growling, snapping, or stiffening may be signs of fear or discomfort, while excessive barking or destructive chewing may indicate boredom or anxiety.

2. **Consult a Professional**: If your Cavalier exhibits consistent aggressive behaviors, such as growling, snapping, or attacking other pets, it's important to consult with a professional dog trainer or behaviorist. A trainer can assess the situation, provide guidance, and help you develop a behavior modification plan that is tailored to your dog's needs.

3. **Positive Reinforcement**: The key to changing undesirable behaviors is positive reinforcement. Reward your Cavalier when they display calm and respectful behavior toward other pets. Use treats, praise, and affection to reinforce good

behavior, rather than punishing bad behavior, which can increase anxiety and fear.

4. **Management and Prevention**: Sometimes, it's necessary to manage situations in a way that prevents aggression or bad behavior. For instance, if your Cavalier has a tendency to be territorial around food, feeding them in a separate area can prevent conflict. Similarly, keeping a safe distance between pets during the early stages of an introduction can help avoid unnecessary tension.

Rough Play or Aggression?

Understanding the difference between rough play and aggression is vital in managing your Cavalier's interactions with other pets. Rough play is typically a normal part of socializing and bonding, but it can sometimes escalate into aggression if boundaries are not established. Here's how to differentiate between the two:

1. **Signs of Rough Play**: During rough play, your Cavalier may jump, run around, or playfully bark, but they will usually show no signs of aggression, such as showing their teeth, growling in an intense way, or lunging. Playful dogs often take breaks, look for cues from the other dog, and have relaxed body language, such as wagging tails or soft eyes.

2. **Signs of Aggression**: Aggression is usually marked by stiff body language, a raised hackle, and intense eye contact. If your Cavalier begins to display these signs, it's important to intervene immediately and separate the dogs. Aggression can lead to injury or escalate into a full-blown fight if not addressed.

3. **Setting Limits**: If you notice your Cavalier getting too rough with another pet, it's important to intervene and set limits. Calmly redirect their attention with a toy or treat and separate them if necessary. Reinforce positive, calm behavior and stop the rough play if it seems to be escalating into aggression.

4. **Socialization is Key**: Proper socialization plays a significant role in teaching your dog appropriate play behavior. The more your Cavalier interacts with other pets in a controlled, positive environment, the better they will learn how to play gently and respect boundaries.

Raising Multiple Puppies From the Same Litter

Raising multiple puppies from the same litter can be a rewarding but challenging experience. While it's possible to raise several Cavalier King Charles Spaniel puppies together, it's essential to be mindful of certain considerations to ensure each puppy's development is not compromised.

1. **Individual Attention**: Each puppy needs individual attention and bonding time with you. Even though they are raised together, it's important to socialize each puppy separately to help them develop into well-adjusted dogs. One-on-one training sessions, playtime, and outings can help you create a strong bond with each puppy.

2. **Avoiding Sibling Rivalry**: Sibling rivalry can sometimes occur when puppies from the same litter are raised together. This can manifest as competition for food, toys, or attention. Ensure that each puppy has their own food bowl, toys, and resting areas to minimize competition and encourage healthy independence.

3. **Proper Socialization**: While it's tempting to let littermates interact with each other constantly, they also need exposure to other dogs, animals, and people outside of the litter. Socializing puppies with a variety of individuals and environments is essential for their development.

4. **Training Challenges**: Multiple puppies from the same litter may develop strong bonds with each other and rely on one another for security, which can make training more challenging. Be patient

and consistent with each puppy, and consider enrolling them in separate training classes to ensure they are receiving the individual attention and socialization they need.

Successfully managing your Cavalier King Charles Spaniel alongside other pets requires patience, consistency, and understanding of each animal's unique needs. Through slow and gradual introductions, positive reinforcement, and careful monitoring of interactions, your Cavalier can develop strong, healthy relationships with other pets in the household. Whether you have other dogs, cats, or smaller animals, creating a harmonious environment for all pets requires commitment but can lead to a rewarding, multi-pet household. Always be prepared to address behavioral challenges, and ensure that each pet gets the individual attention they need to thrive.

CHAPTER 9

Exercising Your Cavalier King Charles Spaniel – Physically and Mentally

The Cavalier King Charles Spaniel, renowned for its charming personality and affectionate nature, is an active and energetic breed despite its small size. They are a breed that thrives on both physical and mental stimulation, which is essential for their health, happiness, and overall well-being. Regular exercise is not just about keeping your dog in good shape—it also helps prevent behavioral problems, reduces anxiety, and strengthens the bond between you and your pet. In this chapter, we will explore the exercise requirements for your Cavalier King Charles Spaniel, discuss how to make exercise enjoyable, and offer tips for keeping your dog mentally engaged to avoid boredom.

Exercise Requirements

Cavalier King Charles Spaniels are generally a healthy breed that enjoys regular physical activity. Although they are small in stature, they have plenty of energy to burn. Exercise helps them stay fit and healthy, but the amount and intensity of exercise can vary based on their age, temperament, and health.

1. **Puppies and Young Cavaliers**: Puppies require frequent short bursts of exercise to keep them healthy and happy, but their bones and joints are still developing, so you must avoid overexerting them. Young Cavaliers usually have a lot of energy and will enjoy playing fetch, exploring the yard, or going on short walks. Aim for 20-30 minutes of exercise daily for puppies under one year of age, spread throughout the day. Over-exercising a puppy can lead to joint issues later in life, so be sure to keep things light and fun.

2. **Adult Cavaliers**: As your Cavalier matures, their exercise needs will increase slightly, but it's essential to maintain a balanced approach. An adult Cavalier typically requires 30-45 minutes of moderate exercise per day. This can include walks, playtime, or agility training. Cavalier King Charles Spaniels enjoy walking, but they also love interactive games like fetch and tug-of-war. Regular exercise helps prevent obesity, which is a common issue in small dog breeds, and it keeps their muscles toned and joints healthy.

3. **Seniors Cavaliers**: Older Cavaliers may slow down, but they still need regular exercise to maintain a healthy weight and prevent muscle atrophy. Shorter, more frequent walks may be a good option for senior dogs, along with gentle play sessions to keep them active. Senior dogs may also benefit from shorter play sessions that focus on brain stimulation, such as puzzle toys or training exercises. As always, it's important to consult your veterinarian about the right amount and intensity of exercise for senior dogs.

4. **Breed-Specific Needs**: The Cavalier King Charles Spaniel is an active breed, but they do not require extreme amounts of exercise like some high-energy breeds. However, because they are prone to obesity and heart issues, it's crucial to ensure they get the proper amount of exercise to maintain their health. Regular cardiovascular exercise, such as brisk walks, helps reduce the risk of heart disease, which Cavaliers can be predisposed to as they age.

5. **Tailoring Exercise to Health Conditions**: Like all breeds, Cavalier King Charles Spaniels can have specific health concerns that may affect their exercise needs. Some may suffer from heart problems like mitral valve disease or joint issues such as patellar luxation. Always tailor the type and intensity of exercise to your dog's individual

health needs. If you notice any signs of discomfort or fatigue, consult with your veterinarian about modifications to their exercise routine.

How to Make Exercise Fun

While Cavaliers need regular physical activity, it's equally important that the exercise is enjoyable for them. Exercise doesn't have to be a chore for your dog; it can be an opportunity to bond, play, and learn new skills. Making exercise fun not only motivates your dog to be more active but also keeps them mentally engaged. Here are some ways to make exercise enjoyable for your Cavalier King Charles Spaniel:

1. **Interactive Games**: Cavaliers love interactive play with their owners. Fetch is one of the most popular games, and it's great for exercise. Throwing a ball or a toy for your Cavalier to chase not only gets them moving but also stimulates their natural instinct to retrieve. You can increase the intensity by adding variations such as hiding the ball for them to find or using multiple balls in a sequence.

2. **Tug-of-War**: Another fun game for Cavaliers is tug-of-war, which helps to burn off energy and engage their muscles. Always remember to let them win occasionally to keep them motivated

and engaged. You can use rope toys or any other sturdy, safe item for tug-of-war. Just make sure to keep it playful and avoid aggressive pulling.

3. **Agility Training**: Cavalier King Charles Spaniels are intelligent dogs that enjoy learning new things. Agility training is an excellent way to combine physical exercise with mental stimulation. You can set up a small agility course in your backyard using cones, tunnels, and hurdles, and guide your dog through it. Not only does this provide physical exercise, but it also keeps their minds sharp as they follow commands and solve problems.

4. **Varied Walks**: Walking is one of the simplest and most effective forms of exercise, but that doesn't mean it has to be boring. Change up your routine by exploring different routes, going to the park, or walking in new environments. Cavalier King Charles Spaniels love to sniff and explore, so allowing them to take in the sights and smells on a leisurely walk is a great way to keep them engaged.

5. **Swimming**: If you have access to a pool, lake, or beach, swimming is another excellent form of low-impact exercise for your Cavalier. Swimming helps strengthen their muscles and joints while being easy on their bones, making it an ideal exercise for dogs with arthritis or joint

issues. Many Cavaliers enjoy the water, especially when it's hot outside, as it provides both cooling and a fun way to exercise.

6. **Playdates**: If your Cavalier enjoys the company of other dogs, arranging playdates with friends, neighbors, or family members can provide great physical and mental stimulation. Socializing with other dogs encourages them to run, chase, and interact in a safe, controlled environment. Just be sure to supervise the interactions, especially when introducing your dog to new dogs for the first time, to ensure the experience is positive.

7. **Enrichment Activities**: Cavalier King Charles Spaniels are highly intelligent, and keeping their minds stimulated is just as important as physical exercise. You can make exercise fun by incorporating mentally challenging activities. Puzzle toys that hide treats, for example, can provide hours of entertainment while encouraging problem-solving. Hide-and-seek games around the house, where your dog has to find a hidden toy or treat, can also be a fun and mentally stimulating way to engage your dog while getting them moving.

Tips for Keeping Your Dog Occupied

While regular physical exercise is essential, keeping your Cavalier King Charles Spaniel mentally stimulated is just as important for their overall happiness. Dogs that are not mentally challenged may develop undesirable behaviors, such as excessive barking, chewing, or digging. Keeping your Cavalier occupied, especially when you're busy or away from home, can help prevent these issues. Here are some tips for keeping your dog entertained:

1. **Rotate Toys**: Just like humans, dogs can get bored with the same toys over time. To keep things interesting, rotate your dog's toys regularly. Keep a few toys out at a time and switch them out every few days. This creates novelty and helps prevent boredom, making each toy feel fresh and exciting.

2. **Puzzle Toys and Treat Dispensers**: Puzzle toys and treat-dispensing toys are great tools for keeping your dog occupied mentally. These toys require your Cavalier to figure out how to get to the treat inside, which engages their problem-solving skills. They can also provide hours of entertainment when you need to keep your dog busy, such as during work hours or when you're out running errands.

3. **Hide Treats Around the House**: If your Cavalier loves using their nose, hide small treats

around the house for them to find. This type of enrichment activity taps into their natural scenting instincts and provides mental stimulation. You can hide treats under rugs, behind doors, or in their bed to make the activity challenging and fun.

4. **Training Sessions**: Training is a fantastic way to keep your Cavalier mentally stimulated. Regular short sessions focused on reinforcing basic commands or teaching new tricks help keep their minds sharp. Cavaliers are quick learners and enjoy having a job to do, so consider incorporating training into your daily routine. Even teaching your dog simple tasks like fetching specific items or rolling over can be a fun way to exercise their brain.

5. **Interactive Games**: Interactive games that require your dog to think or react can provide both mental and physical stimulation. Hide-and-seek games, for example, involve your Cavalier searching for you or a hidden object. You can also play games where your dog has to differentiate between different toys or even learn how to identify certain objects by name.

6. **Puzzle Feeder Bowls**: If your Cavalier tends to eat too quickly or needs extra stimulation during mealtime, consider using a puzzle feeder bowl. These bowls challenge your dog to work for their

food, slowing down the eating process while providing mental stimulation. Puzzle feeders also reduce the likelihood of digestive issues like bloating or indigestion caused by eating too quickly.

Exercising your Cavalier King Charles Spaniel is not only important for their physical health, but it also plays a significant role in their mental well-being. By providing regular, varied physical activities and keeping them mentally engaged with puzzles and training, you'll help ensure that your dog remains healthy, happy, and well-adjusted. Whether it's taking a walk around the neighborhood, playing fetch in the yard, or engaging in some brain-teasing puzzle activities, your Cavalier will appreciate the effort you put into their fitness and mental enrichment. Remember, a tired dog is a happy dog, so keep their body and mind active for a fulfilling life together.

CHAPTER 10

Training Your Cavalier King Charles Spaniel

Training your Cavalier King Charles Spaniel is one of the most rewarding aspects of pet ownership. This breed, known for its affectionate and eager-to-please temperament, is typically responsive to training, making it an excellent companion for families and individuals alike. Proper training is essential not only for good behavior but also for your dog's overall well-being, safety, and integration into your home and community. In this chapter, we will explore the benefits of proper training, methods you can use at home, how to maintain clear expectations, the importance of basic commands, and the different training approaches that work best for this intelligent and friendly breed.

Benefits of Proper Training

The importance of proper training cannot be overstated. For the Cavalier King Charles Spaniel, training is not just about teaching basic commands or correcting behavioral issues; it's about fostering a deep, positive connection between you and your dog. Proper training creates a foundation for mutual understanding and respect, and it helps your dog feel secure in their role within your household. Below are some of the significant benefits of training your Cavalier:

1. **Improved Behavior**: The most obvious benefit of training is better behavior. When trained properly, your Cavalier will understand the house rules and act accordingly. You can avoid common issues like excessive barking, jumping on guests, or destructive chewing. A well-trained dog is more likely to be calm, well-behaved, and easier to manage in social situations.

2. **Strengthened Bond**: Training your dog is a bonding experience that enhances your relationship. The time spent learning together deepens your emotional connection and helps you understand each other's communication styles. A Cavalier King Charles Spaniel is highly responsive to positive reinforcement, making them enthusiastic learners who enjoy spending time with their human family members.

3. **Increased Mental Stimulation**: A key benefit of training is that it keeps your Cavalier mentally stimulated. Cavaliers are intelligent dogs, and without proper mental challenges, they may develop behavioral problems due to boredom.

Regular training sessions provide an outlet for your dog's energy, stimulate their mind, and keep them happy.

4. **Improved Socialization**: Training also helps with socialization, as it teaches your dog how to behave around other people, dogs, and new environments. A well-trained Cavalier is generally more confident and less anxious in unfamiliar situations, making them a pleasure to take on walks, to the vet, or to other social settings.

5. **Safety**: Basic training can be lifesaving, particularly in emergency situations. Commands like "sit," "stay," "come," and "leave it" can help you maintain control over your dog, preventing them from running into dangerous situations such as traffic, or getting into harmful substances.

6. **Prevention of Behavioral Problems**: Without proper training, Cavalier King Charles Spaniels may develop behavioral problems such as separation anxiety, resource guarding, or territorial aggression. Training helps address these issues early on, preventing them from becoming ingrained habits that are harder to correct as your dog matures.

Training Your Cavalier King Charles Spaniel at Home

Training a Cavalier King Charles Spaniel at home is relatively straightforward, thanks to their friendly nature and desire to please their owners. However, consistent training is key to achieving long-term success. Here are some tips for training your Cavalier King Charles Spaniel at home:

1. **Start Early**: The earlier you start training your Cavalier, the better. Puppies have a natural desire to please, and their brains are primed for learning. Beginning training at an early age sets the foundation for good behavior throughout their life. However, even older Cavaliers can learn new tricks and commands—it's never too late to start.

2. **Set a Routine**: Dogs thrive on routine, and consistency is essential for successful training. Set aside time each day for training sessions, ideally in a quiet, distraction-free environment. Short, frequent sessions are more effective than long, drawn-out ones. Aim for about 10-15 minutes of focused training several times a day to keep your dog engaged and prevent frustration.

3. **Use Positive Reinforcement**: Cavalier King Charles Spaniels respond very well to positive reinforcement, so be sure to reward desired behaviors with treats, praise, and affection. When your dog performs a command correctly, offer a

treat and lavish praise. The more you reward good behavior, the more your dog will associate following commands with positive outcomes.

4. **Be Patient and Consistent**: Training takes time, and it's important to be patient with your dog. Cavaliers are quick learners, but they need repetition to fully grasp new concepts. If your dog makes a mistake, don't punish them; instead, gently guide them back on track. Stay calm and consistent in your approach, and your dog will soon learn the desired behavior.

5. **Use Clicker Training**: Clicker training is an excellent way to reinforce desired behavior in Cavalier King Charles Spaniels. A clicker makes a distinct sound when pressed, which serves as a marker for the correct behavior. This method is effective because it provides immediate feedback, which helps your dog understand what they are being rewarded for. Pairing the sound of the clicker with a treat creates a positive association and reinforces the learning process.

Maintaining Clear Expectations

Maintaining clear expectations is essential for successful training. Your dog needs to understand what behaviors are acceptable and which ones are not. Consistency and clarity are key when teaching your Cavalier King Charles Spaniel.

1. **Be Clear and Specific**: When giving commands, be clear and specific. Use the same word for each command every time. For example, use "sit" consistently for the sitting behavior, and don't mix it up with other words like "down." This helps your dog understand what you want them to do.

2. **Establish Boundaries**: It's important to establish boundaries from the beginning. For example, if you don't want your dog on the furniture, make that clear early on. Consistently enforce these boundaries so your dog learns to respect them. If you allow certain behaviors sometimes but not others, it can confuse your dog and make training more difficult.

3. **Avoid Mixed Signals**: Dogs are incredibly perceptive, but they rely on clear, consistent cues to understand their environment. Avoid sending mixed signals, such as rewarding your dog for jumping on guests one day but reprimanding them for it the next. Stay consistent in your responses to certain behaviors, and your dog will learn quickly what's expected of them.

Basic Commands

There are several basic commands every dog should learn, and these are especially important for Cavalier King Charles Spaniels due to their friendly and sometimes excitable nature. The following commands form the foundation of good behavior and communication between you and your dog:

1. **Sit**: The "sit" command is one of the most important and easiest commands to teach. This simple behavior is the starting point for many other commands and is useful for controlling your dog in various situations, such as during walks, when meeting new people, or when you're preparing food.

2. **Stay**: The "stay" command teaches your dog to remain in one place, which can be useful in various situations, such as keeping them out of the way during meals or preventing them from running into dangerous areas.

3. **Come**: The "come" command is essential for recall and ensuring that your dog returns to you when called. This command can be a lifesaver if your dog is ever in a potentially dangerous situation.

4. **Down**: The "down" command helps teach your dog to lie down and remain calm. This command is helpful for settling your dog in different

environments and for situations when you want them to relax.

5. **Leave It**: The "leave it" command teaches your dog to drop or ignore something they are not supposed to have. This command can prevent your dog from ingesting harmful objects or eating something inappropriate.

6. **Heel**: Teaching your Cavalier to walk politely on a leash is important for safety and control. The "heel" command helps your dog walk beside you without pulling or dragging on the leash.

Methods of Training

There are several methods of training, each with its strengths and effectiveness. The following are common approaches for training your Cavalier King Charles Spaniel:

1. **Positive Reinforcement**: Positive reinforcement is the most recommended training method for Cavaliers. It involves rewarding your dog for desirable behaviors, which encourages them to repeat those actions. Use treats, praise, or toys as rewards for good behavior.

2. **Alpha Dog Training**: Some trainers advocate for alpha dog training, where the owner takes on a dominant role to assert authority. However, this method has been largely debunked in favor of

more positive, force-free training techniques. The Cavalier King Charles Spaniel is a gentle, affectionate breed, and overly harsh training methods can be counterproductive.

3. **Clicker Training**: Clicker training uses a clicker sound to mark the correct behavior and is paired with positive reinforcement. This method is effective because it provides clear and immediate feedback, making it easy for your dog to understand what they are being rewarded for.

4. **Lure-Reward Training**: In lure-reward training, you use a treat or toy to guide your dog into the desired position, such as sitting or lying down. Once the dog performs the desired behavior, you reward them with the treat or toy.

Dangers of Negative Reinforcement

Negative reinforcement, which involves the use of punishment or correction to stop unwanted behaviors, is not recommended for training a Cavalier King Charles Spaniel. This method can lead to fear-based behavior, anxiety, and a damaged relationship between you and your dog. Cavalier King Charles Spaniels respond better to positive reinforcement methods, which build trust and cooperation rather than fear.

1. **Fear-Based Training**: Negative reinforcement methods can cause fear and anxiety in your dog,

leading to stress and behavioral problems. This can negatively impact your dog's confidence and cause them to become fearful of you or certain situations.

2. **Breakdown in Communication**: Negative reinforcement can create confusion, as dogs may not understand the connection between their behavior and the punishment. This can lead to frustration for both you and your dog, making training more difficult.

3. **Damage to Bond**: Using punishment-based methods can damage the bond between you and your dog, leading to a breakdown in trust and cooperation. A Cavalier King Charles Spaniel, with its sensitive and affectionate nature, thrives on positive interactions and emotional connection with its owner.

When to Hire a Trainer

While training your Cavalier King Charles Spaniel can be a rewarding experience, there are times when it's beneficial to enlist the help of a professional trainer. If you encounter serious behavioral issues, such as aggression, separation anxiety, or persistent problem behaviors, a trainer can provide expert guidance and tailored solutions. A certified professional dog trainer can also help with advanced training goals, such as therapy dog certification or specialized obedience training.

Training your Cavalier King Charles Spaniel is an essential part of their development and your relationship. Through patience, consistency, and positive reinforcement, you can teach your dog essential commands and behaviors that will enrich both your lives. A well-trained Cavalier will bring immense joy and companionship into your home, while their positive behavior ensures a safe, healthy, and harmonious household.

CHAPTER 11

Traveling with Your Cavalier King Charles Spaniel

Traveling with a Cavalier King Charles Spaniel can be a fun and rewarding experience, but it requires careful planning to ensure your dog's safety, comfort, and well-being. Known for their affectionate nature and adaptability, Cavaliers make excellent travel companions. Whether you're going on a road trip, flying to a new destination, or staying at a hotel, it's important to consider your dog's needs and make the necessary preparations. In this chapter, we'll explore everything you need to know about traveling with your Cavalier King Charles Spaniel, including flying, hotel stays, kenneling, and special tips to ensure smooth and enjoyable trips for both you and your dog.

Flying with Your Dog

Flying with your Cavalier King Charles Spaniel can be an exciting part of your travels, but it requires extra preparation. Some airlines are more accommodating to pets than others, so it's important to research and choose one that provides a pet-friendly experience. Here are some tips to help you navigate flying with your Cavalier King Charles Spaniel:

1. **Check Airline Policies**: Before booking a flight, check the airline's pet policy. Most airlines have specific rules regarding pet travel, such as carrier size requirements, weight limits, and pet fees. Some airlines allow small dogs to travel in the cabin, while others may require them to be checked as cargo. For small breeds like the Cavalier King Charles Spaniel, flying in the cabin is often the best option.

2. **Book Early**: Pet spaces on flights are limited, so it's important to book your flight early to secure a spot for your dog. Airlines often have a limit on the number of pets allowed in the cabin, so early booking gives you the best chance of getting a seat for your Cavalier.

3. **Visit the Veterinarian**: Before flying, take your Cavalier to the vet for a check-up. Make sure your dog is up-to-date on vaccinations and in good health to fly. It's also a good idea to ask your vet for any advice on how to manage your dog's stress during the flight. Some dogs may experience motion sickness or anxiety, so your vet might recommend medication to help your dog stay calm.

4. **Choose the Right Carrier**: The carrier you choose for your Cavalier should be spacious enough for them to stand, turn around, and lie down comfortably. It should also be airline-approved. A soft-sided carrier is often recommended for in-cabin flights, as it can fit under the seat in front of you. Make sure the carrier is well-ventilated and secure, and attach an ID tag with your contact information in case it gets lost.

5. **Prepare Your Dog for Travel**: Before your flight, take your dog on short trips in their career to help them get used to being inside it. This will reduce the chances of them feeling stressed or anxious during the actual flight. On the day of the flight, give your Cavalier a light meal a few hours before departure to avoid any digestive issues during the flight. Avoid giving them a large meal right before travel, as this can lead to discomfort.

6. **Stay Calm and Reassuring**: Dogs can sense their owners' emotions, so it's important to stay calm and positive. Reassure your Cavalier with soft words and gentle petting, but try not to overdo it with affection, as this can sometimes increase anxiety. Once in the air, keep your dog calm by speaking to them softly and offering comfort when necessary.

7. **Hydrate and Take Breaks**: If you are traveling on a long flight, make sure your Cavalier stays hydrated. Bring a small water bottle and a collapsible bowl, and offer your dog water during the flight. Depending on the length of the flight, you may also be able to take your dog out of their carrier during a layover or rest stop.

Hotel Stays with Your Dog

Many hotels now welcome pets, but it's essential to do your research beforehand to ensure a pleasant stay for both you and your Cavalier King Charles Spaniel. Here are some tips for staying in hotels with your dog:

1. **Research Pet-Friendly Hotels**: Not all hotels are pet-friendly, so it's important to check the hotel's pet policy before booking. Some hotels may charge a pet fee or limit the number of pets per room. Others may provide amenities like dog beds, food bowls, and even doggy daycare services. Look for hotels that cater to pet owners, as they are more likely to offer a stress-free environment for both you and your dog.

2. **Book a Pet-Friendly Room**: When booking your room, confirm that it is pet-friendly. Some hotels only have specific rooms or floors designated for pets, so it's important to confirm this with the hotel staff in advance. Additionally, inquire about

any size or breed restrictions to ensure your Cavalier is allowed to stay.

3. **Pack for Your Dog**: When traveling with your dog, be sure to pack everything they may need during your stay. This includes food, water, toys, grooming supplies, and any medications. You may also want to bring your dog's bedding or a favorite blanket to make them feel more at home. If your Cavalier is crate-trained, bringing their crate can provide them with a familiar, safe space during your stay.

4. **Follow Hotel Policies**: When staying in a hotel with your dog, it's important to follow the hotel's pet policies. Keep your Cavalier on a leash when outside the room, and make sure to clean up after them. Be considerate of other guests, and never leave your dog unattended in the room for extended periods of time, especially if they tend to bark or display anxiety when left alone.

5. **Find Dog-Friendly Activities**: Many cities offer dog-friendly parks, trails, and restaurants. Look for local activities or places that welcome dogs, so you and your Cavalier can enjoy your vacation together. Dog-friendly patios, parks, and pet-friendly beaches are perfect for a day of exploration.

Kenneling vs. Dog Sitters

When you're unable to take your Cavalier King Charles Spaniel with you, you'll need to decide whether to use a kennel or hire a dog sitter. Both options have their pros and cons, and it's important to choose the one that best suits your dog's needs.

1. **Kennels**: A kennel provides boarding services for dogs while their owners are away. Many kennels offer amenities such as exercise areas, grooming, and meals. However, not all kennels are created equal, and some may not provide the level of care and attention that your Cavalier needs. When choosing a kennel, visit the facility in advance to ensure it's clean, well-maintained, and staffed with experienced professionals who are familiar with dog behavior.

2. **Dog Sitters**: A dog sitter is a great option for Cavalier King Charles Spaniels, as they can stay in the comfort of their own home while receiving personalized care. Dog sitters can also offer more flexible schedules, such as multiple daily walks or playtime, and provide a more one-on-one experience. You can hire a dog sitter to stay in your home or arrange for someone to visit your dog daily. However, it's important to choose a trusted and experienced sitter, and always check references.

3. **Choosing the Right Option**: The decision between a kennel and a dog sitter will depend on your Cavalier's personality and needs. If your dog is more independent and enjoys socializing with other dogs, a kennel may be a good option. However, if your dog is more sensitive or anxious, a dog sitter who can offer individualized care may be the better choice. Consider your dog's temperament, any medical needs, and how comfortable they are with new environments when making your decision.

Choosing the Right Boarding Facility

If you decide that boarding your Cavalier is the best option, it's crucial to choose the right facility to ensure your dog's safety, comfort, and well-being. Here are some factors to consider when selecting a boarding facility:

1. **Reputation**: Look for a boarding facility with a strong reputation for providing quality care for pets. Ask for recommendations from friends, family, or your veterinarian. Read online reviews and check the facility's ratings with organizations like the Better Business Bureau.
2. **Tour the Facility**: Before booking a stay, visit the boarding facility in person to see the conditions firsthand. Check that the facility is

clean, well-lit, and well-ventilated. Ensure that the staff is friendly, knowledgeable, and experienced with dogs, and ask about their policies regarding feeding, exercise, and emergency care.

3. **Staff-to-Dog Ratio**: A good boarding facility should have a low staff-to-dog ratio, ensuring that each dog receives the individual attention they need. Make sure the staff members are trained in dog behavior and first aid and that there are enough people on hand to supervise and care for the dogs at all times.

4. **Health and Safety**: Ensure that the boarding facility follows strict health and safety protocols, including vaccinations and parasite control. Ask about their procedures for dealing with medical emergencies and whether they have a relationship with a local veterinarian.

5. **Special Needs**: If your Cavalier has any special medical needs or requires extra care, be sure to discuss these with the facility. Some boarding facilities offer special services such as medication administration, dietary accommodations, or individualized care for dogs with anxiety or other behavioral issues.

Special Tips and Tricks for Traveling

1. **Keep Your Dog Calm**: Traveling can be stressful for dogs, especially if it's their first time on the road or in the air. To help keep your Cavalier calm, provide familiar items such as their favorite toy, blanket, or bed. This can offer comfort and help reduce anxiety during travel.
2. **Hydration and Food**: Make sure your dog stays hydrated and fed during travel. Bring along water and a collapsible bowl for easy access, and plan your trip to allow for rest breaks and bathroom stops.
3. **Routine and Familiarity**: Dogs thrive on routine, so try to maintain their feeding, walking, and bathroom schedules as much as possible. Familiar scents and routines will help your Cavalier feel more at ease during your travels.
4. **Use a Pet Tracker**: To keep track of your dog during travel, consider using a pet tracker collar. This can provide peace of mind in case your dog gets lost or separated from you.

Traveling with your Cavalier King Charles Spaniel can be an enjoyable experience, provided that you take the time to plan and prepare. Whether you're flying, staying in a hotel, or exploring new places together, your dog's safety, comfort, and happiness should always be a priority. By following these tips and making the necessary arrangements, you can ensure that both you and your Cavalier have a stress-free and enjoyable trip every time you travel.

CHAPTER 12

Grooming Your Cavalier King Charles Spaniel

Cavalier King Charles Spaniels are known for their luxurious, silky coats that require regular grooming to maintain their beauty and health. Their long, flowing fur can easily become tangled or matted without proper care, and neglecting grooming can lead to discomfort, skin irritations, and even infections. As a responsible dog owner, understanding how to groom your Cavalier is essential to ensuring they remain comfortable and well-maintained. In this chapter, we will cover the basics of grooming your Cavalier King Charles Spaniel, from coat care and brushing techniques to ear cleaning and dental hygiene.

Coat Basics

The Cavalier King Charles Spaniel has a medium-length, silky coat that is soft to the touch, with feathers on the legs, ears, and tail. Their coat comes in several color patterns, including Blenheim (chestnut and white), tricolor (black, tan, and white), ruby (solid red), and black and tan. Despite the beauty of their coat, Cavaliers shed regularly, particularly during shedding seasons (spring and fall), and require consistent grooming to prevent their fur from becoming tangled or matted.

It's important to note that while the Cavalier King Charles Spaniel is often classified as a low-shedding breed, their hair requires regular attention to keep it looking its best. Their coat is not a simple "wash-and-go" affair, and without proper care, the fine, silky fur can become tangled, leading to mats that are not only unsightly but can also cause skin irritations and discomfort for your dog.

Basic Grooming Tools

To properly groom your Cavalier King Charles Spaniel, you will need a selection of grooming tools designed to keep their coat healthy and looking great. The essential tools for grooming a Cavalier include:

1. **Slicker Brush**: A slicker brush is a must-have for Cavaliers. It helps detangle and remove loose fur, preventing mats from forming. It's especially useful for the feathers on the tail, legs, and ears. Choose a brush with fine, flexible pins to avoid causing any irritation or scratching on your dog's skin.

2. **Pin Brush**: A pin brush is another tool to help with coat maintenance. It's excellent for gently removing tangles and mats in your Cavalier's long hair without causing breakage. A pin brush is particularly useful for fine coats like those of the Cavalier King Charles Spaniel.
3. **Wide-tooth Comb**: A wide-tooth comb is ideal for detangling areas that are more prone to mats, such as the ears, armpits, and underbelly. Use it after brushing to ensure you've removed all tangles and mats.
4. **Nail Clippers**: Regular nail trimming is an essential part of grooming your Cavalier. Long nails can be painful for your dog and can lead to problems such as difficulty walking or even joint issues over time. A good pair of nail clippers designed for dogs will make this task easier and safer.
5. **Ear Cleaning Solution**: Cavaliers are prone to ear infections due to their long, floppy ears that can trap moisture and debris. Regular ear cleaning helps prevent infections. Choose a gentle ear cleaning solution made for dogs and cotton balls or pads to clean their ears.
6. **Toothbrush and Dog Toothpaste**: Oral hygiene is often overlooked in pet care, but it's an important aspect of your dog's overall health. Using a soft-bristled toothbrush and canine-safe

toothpaste will help prevent plaque buildup, tartar, and gum disease.

7. **Shampoo and Conditioner**: Cavalier King Charles Spaniels require special attention when it comes to bathing. Use a mild, dog-specific shampoo to avoid irritating your dog's skin. You can also use a dog conditioner to keep the coat soft and manageable. Avoid human shampoos, as they can disrupt the natural pH balance of your dog's skin.

Bathing and Brushing

Cavalier King Charles Spaniels don't need to be bathed too often, as over-bathing can strip their coat of essential oils that help keep their skin moisturized. Typically, bathing every 4 to 6 weeks is sufficient, but this can vary depending on how active your dog is and how much time they spend outdoors.

Here's how to bathe and brush your Cavalier King Charles Spaniel:

1. **Brush Before Bathing**: Always brush your dog's coat before bathing. This helps to remove tangles and mats, which can become even more difficult to handle once wet. Use a slicker brush to remove any loose fur and detangle the coat.

2. **Prepare the Bath**: Ensure the water temperature is lukewarm—not too hot or cold. Fill the tub or sink with just enough water to wet your dog's coat. If you're using a bathtub, place a non-slip mat in the bottom to prevent your Cavalier from slipping.

3. **Shampooing**: Apply a small amount of dog-specific shampoo to your dog's coat and gently massage it in. Be sure to avoid getting shampoo in your dog's eyes, ears, or mouth. Thoroughly rinse the shampoo out to prevent residue from irritating your dog's skin.

4. **Conditioning**: After rinsing out the shampoo, you can apply a dog conditioner if desired. This helps to keep your Cavalier's coat soft and shiny. Be sure to rinse thoroughly after applying the conditioner.

5. **Drying**: Towel-dry your Cavalier after the bath to remove excess moisture. Cavaliers have long coats that can take a while to dry, so you may also want to use a hairdryer on a low, cool setting to help speed up the drying process. Be sure to keep the dryer at a safe distance to avoid overheating your dog.

6. **Final Brushing**: Once your Cavalier is dry, give them one final brush to ensure the coat is smooth and free of tangles. Pay special attention to areas

that are prone to matting, such as behind the ears, the tail, and under the legs.

Nail Trimming

Keeping your Cavalier's nails trimmed is crucial for their health and comfort. Long nails can cause pain when walking, and they can even lead to joint issues over time. Regular nail trimming is important to prevent this.

1. **Trimming Tools**: Use dog nail clippers or a nail grinder specifically designed for dogs. Avoid using human nail clippers, as they can cause injury to your dog's nails.
2. **How to Trim**: Hold your Cavalier's paw gently and examine the nail to identify the "quick," which is the pinkish area that contains blood vessels. Avoid cutting into the quick, as this can cause bleeding. Trim the nail a small amount at a time to avoid cutting too much.
3. **Frequency**: Trim your dog's nails every 3 to 4 weeks or as needed. If you hear your dog's nails clicking on the floor when they walk, it's time for a trim.

Cleaning the Ears and Eyes

Cavalier King Charles Spaniels are prone to ear infections due to their long, floppy ears. It's essential to clean their ears regularly to remove excess wax, dirt, and moisture. Similarly, the breed is also prone to eye issues, so cleaning around their eyes is necessary to prevent irritation and infections.

1. **Ear Cleaning**: Use a veterinarian-recommended ear cleaning solution. Gently lift your dog's ear flap and apply the solution to the ear canal. Massage the base of the ear to distribute the solution and loosen any dirt. Use a cotton ball or gauze to wipe away the debris. Never use cotton swabs in your dog's ears, as they can push debris further into the ear canal.

2. **Eye Cleaning**: Cavalier King Charles Spaniels can develop tear stains around their eyes, especially if they have longer hair. To clean around the eyes, use a damp cotton ball to wipe away any discharge. Be sure to use a gentle, pet-safe eye cleanser to avoid irritation.

Dental Care

Dental hygiene is just as important for dogs as it is for humans. Regular brushing can help prevent bad breath, gum disease, and tartar buildup. Here's how to maintain your Cavalier King Charles Spaniel's dental health:

1. **Tooth Brushing**: Use a soft-bristled toothbrush and dog-safe toothpaste to brush your dog's teeth.

Start slowly, gradually getting your dog used to the sensation of having their teeth brushed. Focus on the outside surfaces of the teeth, where plaque tends to build up. Aim to brush your dog's teeth several times a week.

2. **Dental Chews**: In addition to regular brushing, dental chews can help reduce tartar buildup and keep your dog's teeth clean. Be sure to choose dental chews that are appropriate for your dog's size and breed.

When to Seek Professional Help

While regular grooming is essential for your Cavalier King Charles Spaniel, there are times when you may need to seek professional help:

1. **Severe Matting**: If your dog's coat becomes severely matted and you're unable to detangle it yourself, it may be necessary to visit a professional groomer. Matting can cause discomfort and even skin issues, so it's important to address it promptly.

2. **Ear Infections**: If your dog shows signs of an ear infection, such as excessive scratching, head shaking, or a foul odor from the ears, consult your veterinarian. Infections can be painful and require professional treatment.

3. **Dental Problems**: If your Cavalier's breath becomes excessively foul, they have difficulty chewing, or their gums appear red or swollen, it may be time for a veterinary dental cleaning.
4. **Nail Problems**: If you're unable to trim your dog's nails safely, or if your Cavalier has injured their nails, it's best to seek help from a veterinarian or professional groomer.

Grooming your Cavalier King Charles Spaniel is an essential part of responsible pet ownership. By following these grooming tips and maintaining a regular schedule, you can ensure that your dog remains healthy, comfortable, and happy. Regular grooming will also help strengthen the bond between you and your Cavalier, as it's a great opportunity for you to spend quality time together and ensure their well-being.

CHAPTER 13

Basic Health Care

As a responsible Cavalier King Charles Spaniel owner, one of your most important duties is to ensure that your dog maintains good health throughout their life. Regular veterinary visits, proper preventive care, and awareness of common health issues are all essential for keeping your Cavalier in top condition. In this chapter, we will explore the basics of health care for your Cavalier King Charles Spaniel, covering everything from routine veterinary visits and vaccinations to parasite prevention, holistic treatments, and pet insurance. Understanding how to care for your dog's health will not only improve their quality of life but also ensure they remain happy and comfortable as they age.

Visiting the Vet

Routine visits to the vet are one of the cornerstones of preventive health care for your Cavalier King Charles Spaniel. Regular check-ups allow your veterinarian to monitor your dog's overall health, detect potential issues early, and ensure that your dog is up to date on their vaccinations and preventive treatments.

Your dog should have their first veterinary visit shortly after you bring them home. This initial visit is usually focused on a general health assessment, vaccinations, and parasite prevention. Your vet will check for any early signs of common health conditions, such as heart murmurs (which Cavaliers are prone to), patellar luxation, and dental issues. It's also an opportunity to ask any questions about your dog's diet, behavior, and development.

After this initial check-up, routine visits should continue throughout your dog's life. Typically, puppies will need to visit the vet every few months for vaccinations and check-ups, while adult dogs should be seen annually or biannually. Senior dogs may require more frequent visits to monitor age-related conditions.

Fleas and Ticks

Fleas and ticks are common pests that can cause significant health problems for your Cavalier King Charles Spaniel if left untreated. Fleas are small, parasitic insects that live on your dog's skin and feed on their blood. In addition to the irritation they cause, fleas can also transmit diseases, including flea allergy dermatitis, which can result in itchy, inflamed skin.

Ticks, which latch onto your dog's skin to feed on their blood, can transmit serious diseases such as Lyme disease and Ehrlichiosis.

To prevent flea and tick infestations, it's important to use a reliable, veterinarian-approved flea and tick prevention product. These come in various forms, including topical treatments, oral medications, and collars. Your veterinarian can help you choose the best flea and tick prevention method for your Cavalier based on factors like their age, lifestyle, and the area in which you live.

If you notice signs of fleas or ticks, such as excessive scratching, hair loss, or the presence of small, dark specks (flea dirt) or ticks attached to the skin, contact your vet for guidance. In some cases, a thorough flea bath and the application of topical treatments may be necessary to clear up the infestation.

Intestinal Worms and Parasites

Intestinal worms, including roundworms, hookworms, tapeworms, and whipworms, are common in dogs, especially puppies. These parasites can cause symptoms such as vomiting, diarrhea, weight loss, and lethargy. While these parasites are treatable with medications prescribed by your vet, it's important to take preventive measures to avoid infestations in the first place.

Most veterinarians recommend deworming puppies starting at 2 weeks of age, with follow-up treatments at 4, 6, and 8 weeks. Adult dogs should be dewormed regularly, typically once or twice a year, depending on their risk factors. Puppies and dogs that spend a lot of time outdoors or come into contact with other animals may need more frequent deworming.

Additionally, routine stool tests can help detect intestinal parasites. If your Cavalier has symptoms of intestinal worms, such as diarrhea or weight loss, visit your veterinarian for a fecal exam and appropriate treatment.

Vaccinations

Vaccination is a vital part of your dog's overall health care plan. Vaccines protect your Cavalier from potentially serious and contagious diseases, including parvovirus, distemper, rabies, and kennel cough. These diseases can cause severe illness, long-term health problems, and even death.

Puppies should receive a series of vaccinations starting at around 6 to 8 weeks of age, with booster shots every 3 to 4 weeks until they are about 16 weeks old. After the initial series of vaccines, adult dogs typically receive boosters every 1 to 3 years, depending on the specific vaccine and the recommendations of your vet.

Rabies vaccinations are required by law in many areas, and your vet will ensure that your dog receives this critical vaccine at the appropriate time. It's important to keep track of vaccination schedules and ensure your dog's vaccinations are up to date.

Common Diseases and Conditions

Cavalier King Charles Spaniels are prone to certain hereditary health issues. As a responsible pet owner, it's essential to be aware of these conditions and monitor your dog's health regularly for any signs or symptoms.

1. **Mitral Valve Disease (MVD)**: MVD is a heart condition that affects many Cavalier King Charles Spaniels, especially as they age. It occurs when the mitral valve in the heart doesn't close properly, leading to heart murmurs, fluid buildup, and heart failure. Regular veterinary check-ups, including heart screenings, can help detect MVD early, allowing for better management of the condition.

2. **Syringomyelia**: Syringomyelia is a painful neurological condition that affects the brain and spinal cord. It's relatively common in Cavaliers and can cause symptoms such as head tilting, whining, sensitivity to touch, and weakness. If your Cavalier shows signs of pain or discomfort

in their neck or head, it's important to seek veterinary care immediately.

3. **Patellar Luxation**: This condition occurs when the kneecap (patella) slips out of its normal position. It can lead to lameness and difficulty walking. Patellar luxation is a hereditary condition, and early detection can help manage the symptoms and prevent further damage.

4. **Eye Problems**: Cavaliers are also prone to several eye conditions, including cataracts, retinal problems, and dry eye. Regular eye exams by a veterinarian can help detect these issues early, ensuring prompt treatment.

It's important to be proactive in your dog's health care and regularly monitor them for any unusual symptoms. If your Cavalier shows signs of pain, lethargy, or behavioral changes, consult your veterinarian promptly.

Holistic Alternatives and Supplements

In addition to conventional veterinary care, many Cavalier King Charles Spaniel owners seek holistic treatments to support their dog's health. While these alternatives should not replace traditional veterinary care, they can be used alongside conventional treatments to improve your dog's overall well-being.

1. **Herbs**: Some herbs can have beneficial effects on your dog's health. For example, turmeric has anti-inflammatory properties that can help manage arthritis or joint discomfort. Milk thistle is often used as a liver detoxifier, and echinacea can boost the immune system. Always consult your veterinarian before adding any herbal supplements to your dog's diet to ensure they are safe and appropriate for your Cavalier.

2. **CBD Oil**: CBD oil has become increasingly popular as a natural remedy for pets, particularly for managing anxiety, pain, and inflammation. Some studies suggest that CBD oil can help reduce the symptoms of arthritis, alleviate anxiety, and support overall well-being in dogs. However, it's important to use only high-quality CBD products made specifically for pets. Always discuss CBD oil use with your veterinarian to ensure the proper dosage and avoid any potential interactions with other medications.

Pet Insurance

Pet insurance is an invaluable resource for Cavalier King Charles Spaniel owners who want to protect their dog's health while managing the costs of veterinary care. Veterinary bills can be expensive, particularly if your dog develops a chronic condition or requires emergency treatment. Pet insurance can help reduce the financial burden and ensure that your dog receives the best care possible.

There are several types of pet insurance plans available, including accident-only coverage, illness-only coverage, and comprehensive plans that cover both accidents and illnesses. Some plans also offer coverage for preventive care, such as vaccinations, wellness exams, and routine dental cleanings. When choosing a pet insurance provider, be sure to compare policies, premiums, deductibles, and coverage options to find the plan that best suits your needs.

Basic health care for your Cavalier King Charles Spaniel involves a combination of preventive care, regular veterinary visits, proper nutrition, and awareness of common health issues. By being proactive in your dog's health care and maintaining a strong relationship with your veterinarian, you can help ensure that your Cavalier leads a long, healthy, and happy life. Whether it's flea and tick prevention, vaccinations, or holistic treatments, every step you take to care for your dog will contribute to their overall well-being and happiness.

CHAPTER 14

Nutrition

As a pet owner, one of the most significant ways you can ensure the long-term health and happiness of your Cavalier King Charles Spaniel is by providing them with the right nutrition. Nutrition plays a crucial role in your dog's growth, energy levels, coat condition, immune system, and overall well-being. A healthy diet not only prevents obesity and promotes a healthy weight but also reduces the risk of diseases like diabetes, heart disease, and joint issues.

In this chapter, we will explore the different aspects of feeding your Cavalier King Charles Spaniel, including the benefits of quality dog food, the types of commercial foods available, what ingredients to watch out for, homemade dog food options, and the importance of weight management. Understanding the nutritional needs of your dog is essential for their health and longevity, and the right diet can help them thrive.

Benefits of Quality Dog Food

The benefits of high-quality dog food are immense. Dogs, especially Cavalier King Charles Spaniels, who are predisposed to certain health conditions such as heart disease and joint issues, can benefit significantly from a nutritious, well-balanced diet. Quality dog food provides the essential nutrients needed for optimal growth, development, and maintenance of a healthy body.

1. **Healthier Coat and Skin**: A balanced diet rich in omega-3 and omega-6 fatty acids can contribute to a shiny, healthy coat and healthy skin. These fatty acids help maintain the skin's moisture barrier, preventing dryness and flakiness, which is particularly important for a breed like the Cavalier, which has a longer, silky coat that can be prone to tangling and matting.

2. **Stronger Immune System**: High-quality dog food contains essential vitamins, minerals, and antioxidants that help support your dog's immune system. These nutrients can help protect against illnesses and improve the overall health of your Cavalier, keeping them active and strong.

3. **Joint and Bone Health**: Cavalier King Charles Spaniels can be prone to joint issues like patellar luxation and hip dysplasia. High-quality food that contains glucosamine and chondroitin can help support joint health and mobility, ensuring that your dog can enjoy a comfortable and active life.

4. **Better Digestion**: Premium dog foods are typically formulated with easily digestible ingredients that promote good gut health and regular bowel movements. They often include fiber sources like sweet potatoes, pumpkins, or beet pulp to aid digestion, which is important for your dog's overall health and well-being.
5. **Sustained Energy Levels**: Dogs that are fed a nutritious diet tend to have stable energy levels, which means they are more likely to be active, engaged, and happy. A balanced diet helps regulate blood sugar levels, ensuring that your dog has the energy to play, exercise, and enjoy their daily activities.
6. **Longer Life Expectancy**: High-quality dog food contributes to a dog's overall health, which can lead to a longer, healthier life. A well-balanced diet, combined with exercise and regular veterinary care, can help prevent many of the common health problems that affect dogs, leading to a longer and more fulfilling life.

Types of Commercial Dog Foods

When it comes to commercial dog food, there are several options available. Each type of dog food has its own benefits and may be more suitable depending on your Cavalier King Charles Spaniel's age, activity level, and any specific health concerns. The most common types of commercial dog food are:

1. **Dry Dog Food (Kibble)**: Dry dog food is one of the most popular and convenient types of dog food. Kibble is available in a wide variety of formulas, including breed-specific, age-specific, and condition-specific options. It is cost-effective, has a long shelf life, and is easy to store. The crunchiness of kibble also helps maintain dental health by scraping plaque from your dog's teeth. However, not all dry dog foods are created equal, and some may be filled with low-quality ingredients or fillers, so it's important to choose a high-quality brand.

2. **Canned Dog Food**: Canned dog food, or wet food, is a good option for dogs that are picky eaters or have difficulty chewing dry food. Wet food is often higher in protein and fat than kibble and can be a great choice for underweight dogs or dogs with higher energy needs. However, it's important to choose a wet food that is free from unnecessary fillers and low-quality meats. Canned food also tends to be more expensive and has a shorter shelf life compared to kibble.

3. **Raw Dog Food**: Raw dog food, often called a "raw diet" or "BARF" (Biologically Appropriate Raw Food) diet, is based on the idea of feeding

dogs foods that are closer to what they would eat in the wild, such as raw meat, bones, fruits, and vegetables. Advocates of raw feeding believe it promotes better health, including improved digestion, healthier skin and coat, and increased energy. However, raw feeding requires careful attention to balance and safety, as improper handling can lead to contamination and nutritional imbalances. Consult your veterinarian before switching to a raw food diet.

4. **Dehydrated Dog Food**: Dehydrated dog food is a more recent option that combines convenience with the benefits of a raw or homemade diet. This type of food is made by removing moisture from natural ingredients, and it often requires you to add water before feeding. Dehydrated food tends to be more nutritious than traditional dry kibble and can provide more natural ingredients. However, it is generally more expensive and may not be as widely available as kibble or canned food.

Ingredients to Watch Out For

When choosing commercial dog food, it's important to read the ingredients list carefully. Some ingredients are beneficial for your dog's health, while others should be avoided. Here are some key ingredients to watch out for:

1. **High-Quality Animal Protein**: Look for named animal proteins such as chicken, turkey, lamb, or beef as the first ingredient. Avoid foods that list "meat by-products" or "animal meal" as the main source of protein, as these can be low-quality and less nutritious.

2. **Grain-Free Ingredients**: While many dogs do well on grain-inclusive diets, some Cavaliers may have sensitivities to grains like wheat, corn, and soy. If your dog has digestive issues or allergies, consider choosing a grain-free food that uses quality carbohydrates like sweet potatoes, peas, or lentils.

3. **Filler Ingredients**: Avoid dog foods that contain large amounts of fillers, such as corn, wheat, soy, or by-products. These ingredients are often included to bulk up the food but provide little nutritional value for your dog.

4. **Artificial Additives**: Stay away from dog foods that contain artificial colors, flavors, or preservatives, such as BHA, BHT, or ethoxyquin. These chemicals can have negative effects on your dog's health and are best avoided.

5. **Excessive Fat or Sugar**: High-fat and high-sugar content in dog food can lead to obesity, diabetes, and other health issues. Look for foods that are balanced and contain healthy fats like omega-3

and omega-6 fatty acids, as well as moderate amounts of carbohydrates.

Categories of Dog Food

Dog food can be categorized based on the specific needs of your dog, such as their age, size, and health condition. Here are the most common categories of dog food:

1. **Puppy Food**: Puppy food is specially formulated to meet the nutritional needs of growing dogs. It contains higher levels of protein, fat, and calories to support healthy development. Since Cavaliers are a small to medium-sized breed, they require food that is rich in nutrients to help them grow strong and healthy.
2. **Adult Dog Food**: Adult dog food is designed to maintain the health and weight of fully grown dogs. It typically contains balanced amounts of protein, fat, and fiber. Since Cavaliers are prone to obesity, it's important to choose an adult food that helps manage their weight and maintain a healthy body condition.
3. **Senior Dog Food**: Senior dog food is formulated to support the specific needs of older dogs, such as joint health, digestive support, and weight management. Since Cavaliers are prone to heart and joint issues, choosing senior food for aging

dogs is a great way to ensure they maintain their health as they age.

4. **Weight Management Food**: If your Cavalier is overweight, weight management food can help them lose weight gradually while still providing the necessary nutrients. These foods typically have fewer calories and a higher fiber content to help your dog feel full without overfeeding.

Homemade Dog Food

Some pet owners prefer to make homemade dog food for their pets to have more control over the ingredients. Homemade dog food can be a healthy alternative, provided that you carefully balance nutrients and ensure that your dog gets all the essential vitamins, minerals, and amino acids they need.

A balanced homemade diet for your Cavalier King Charles Spaniel should include a mix of lean protein (such as chicken, turkey, or beef), vegetables (such as carrots, spinach, or sweet potatoes), and healthy fats (such as fish oil or flaxseed oil). However, preparing homemade dog food requires careful planning and an understanding of your dog's nutritional needs. It's recommended that you consult with your veterinarian or a pet nutritionist before making the transition to homemade meals.

Table Food – What Is Good, What Is Not?

Many dog owners wonder if it's okay to share their own food with their pets. While some human foods are safe for dogs in moderation, others can be toxic or harmful. For example:

- **Safe foods**: Apples (without seeds), carrots, lean meats, sweet potatoes, and plain rice.
- **Foods to avoid**: Chocolate, onions, garlic, grapes, raisins, avocados, and foods with high sugar or salt content.

Always ensure that the food you offer your dog is appropriate for their dietary needs and doesn't pose a health risk.

Weight Management

Maintaining a healthy weight is particularly important for Cavalier King Charles Spaniels, as they are prone to obesity. Excess weight puts stress on their joints, heart, and overall health. To keep your Cavalier at a healthy weight, monitor their food intake, feed them high-quality food, and provide regular exercise. If you are concerned about your dog's weight, consult with your veterinarian for personalized recommendations.

Proper nutrition is essential to the health and well-being of your Cavalier King Charles Spaniel. By providing them with high-quality commercial dog food or carefully prepared homemade meals, you can ensure that they have the nutrients they need to thrive. Make informed decisions about the food you feed your dog, paying attention to ingredient quality, portion sizes, and your dog's specific needs. By managing their diet and weight, you can help your Cavalier live a long, healthy, and active life.

CHAPTER 15

Dealing with Unwanted Behaviors

Dealing with unwanted behaviors in your Cavalier King Charles Spaniel can be one of the most challenging aspects of dog ownership. While this breed is known for its affectionate nature, intelligence, and friendly demeanor, like all dogs, Cavaliers can develop habits or behaviors that are undesirable. Understanding the nature of these behaviors, how to address them, and when to seek professional help is crucial in ensuring a harmonious relationship between you and your dog.

In this chapter, we will delve into the most common behavioral issues faced by Cavalier King Charles Spaniels, how to identify and address them, and strategies for effectively managing unwanted behaviors. We will also explore when it's time to call in a professional to help resolve persistent problems. With patience, consistency, and the right approach, most undesirable behaviors can be corrected, leading to a well-behaved and happy companion.

What is Considered Bad Behavior?

Before we can address unwanted behaviors, it's important to define what constitutes bad behavior. What one owner might consider undesirable, another might see as just a phase or a normal part of a dog's development. However, there are certain behaviors that are generally recognized as problematic and should be corrected for the well-being of both the dog and the owner.

Common examples of bad behavior in Cavalier King Charles Spaniels (and dogs in general) include:

1. **Excessive Barking**: While some barking is natural for dogs, excessive barking can be a nuisance to both the dog and the household. Barking for attention, out of boredom, or in response to noises outside the home can disrupt your day and your neighbors.

2. **Separation Anxiety**: Cavaliers are known for their strong attachment to their owners. However, if your dog experiences severe distress when left alone, resulting in destructive behaviors like chewing, howling, or accidents inside the house, it may be a sign of separation anxiety.

3. **Chewing**: Puppies are naturally inclined to chew, especially when they are teething, but excessive chewing on inappropriate objects like furniture, shoes, or wires is a common problem. Left unaddressed, this behavior can lead to costly damage in your home.

4. **Jumping on People**: Cavalier King Charles Spaniels are affectionate and love attention. However, jumping up on people, especially visitors, can be a disruptive behavior, particularly when the dog is excited or overstimulated.

5. **Pulling on the Leash**: While Cavaliers are typically well-behaved on walks, some may pull on the leash, making walks less enjoyable for you both. This behavior can develop if the dog has not been properly trained to walk politely on a leash.

6. **Food Aggression**: Although rare in Cavaliers, some dogs can develop food aggression, where they growl, snap, or show signs of possessiveness over their food. This can be a serious issue, particularly if there are children in the home or other pets.

7. **Aggression Towards Other Animals**: While Cavaliers are generally social and friendly with other pets, some may display aggressive behavior, especially if they feel threatened or territorial. This can manifest as growling, snapping, or even attacking other animals in the household or outside.

8. **Digging**: Digging can be a sign of boredom, anxiety, or a natural instinct, especially in puppies. However, if left unaddressed, it can become a habit that damages your yard or home.

Finding the Root of the Problem

One of the first steps in addressing unwanted behaviors is to understand what is causing them. Dogs do not misbehave for no reason—there is almost always an underlying cause. Some common reasons for unwanted behaviors in Cavalier King Charles Spaniels include:

1. **Lack of Proper Training**: Cavalier King Charles Spaniels are intelligent dogs, but they need consistent training and boundaries. Without proper guidance, they may develop bad habits. Training should start early and be ongoing throughout their lives to ensure they understand the rules.

2. **Boredom and Lack of Stimulation**: Cavalier King Charles Spaniels are active and social dogs that need regular exercise and mental stimulation. If they do not receive enough physical activity or mental challenges, they may engage in destructive behaviors like chewing, digging, or barking out of boredom.

3. **Separation Anxiety**: As a breed known for being particularly attached to their owners, Cavaliers are more likely to experience separation anxiety. When left alone for too long, they may display destructive behaviors such as chewing, howling, or having accidents inside the house.

4. **Health Issues**: Sometimes, bad behaviors can be linked to physical discomfort or health problems. If your dog suddenly begins displaying unwanted behaviors, such as excessive barking, aggression, or changes in behavior, it's important to rule out any underlying health conditions.

5. **Unclear Communication**: Inconsistent rules and commands can confuse your dog. If different members of the household provide different cues or expectations, your dog may become unsure of how to behave. Clear, consistent communication is essential for effective behavior management.

6. **Lack of Socialization**: Cavalier King Charles Spaniels are typically friendly and social, but if they have not been properly socialized, they may develop fear-based behaviors such as aggression towards strangers or other pets. Socialization should start early and continue throughout their lives.

How to Properly Correct Your Dog

Correcting unwanted behaviors requires a combination of patience, consistency, and the right techniques. The key to successful behavior modification is using positive reinforcement methods while avoiding punishment, which can lead to fear and anxiety.

1. **Positive Reinforcement**: One of the most effective ways to correct unwanted behavior is to use positive reinforcement. This means rewarding your dog with treats, praise, or playtime when they exhibit good behavior. Over time, they will learn that good behavior leads to positive outcomes, while bad behavior results in no reward.

2. **Redirecting Behavior**: Instead of punishing bad behavior, redirect your dog's attention to a more appropriate activity. For example, if your dog is chewing on furniture, redirect them to a chew toy. If they're barking excessively, provide a command like "quiet" and reward them when they stop barking.

3. **Setting Clear Boundaries**: It's essential to establish clear boundaries for your dog and stick to them consistently. If jumping on people is not allowed, don't allow it, even once in a while. Consistency is key in ensuring your dog understands what is expected of them.

4. **Providing Mental and Physical Stimulation**: To prevent boredom-induced behaviors, provide your dog with plenty of physical exercise and mental stimulation. Regular walks, playtime, and interactive toys can help keep your Cavalier mentally and physically engaged.

5. **Desensitization and Counterconditioning**: For dogs that exhibit anxiety or aggression, desensitization and counterconditioning can be effective. This involves gradually exposing your dog to the triggers of their anxiety or aggression in a controlled environment and rewarding calm behavior. Over time, they will learn to associate these triggers with positive experiences.

6. **Training Sessions**: Consistent training sessions are essential in correcting unwanted behaviors. Short, positive sessions (5-10 minutes) every day are more effective than long, exhausting sessions. Be sure to use treats and praise to reinforce good behavior and encourage your dog to stay focused.

When to Call a Professional

While most unwanted behaviors can be corrected with time and training, there are some cases where it may be necessary to seek professional help. If you are struggling to address persistent behavioral issues or if your dog's behavior is dangerous, consulting a professional dog trainer or behaviorist can provide valuable insights and techniques.

1. **Severe Aggression**: If your dog is showing signs of aggression towards humans or other pets, it's crucial to seek help immediately. Aggressive behavior can be dangerous and requires a trained

professional to assess the situation and provide a behavior modification plan.

2. **Separation Anxiety**: Dogs with severe separation anxiety can exhibit destructive behaviors such as tearing up furniture, excessively barking, or even injuring themselves when left alone. A professional can help develop a desensitization plan to reduce the anxiety and improve your dog's comfort with being alone.

3. **Phobias or Extreme Fears**: Some dogs develop extreme phobias or fears of certain situations, people, or objects. A behaviorist can help identify the root cause of the fear and work with you to modify the behavior through gradual exposure and positive reinforcement.

4. **Inconsistent Progress**: If you have been working on a behavioral issue for a while and have not seen progress, it may be time to seek professional help. A dog trainer or behaviorist can provide new techniques and strategies that may be more effective.

5. **Health-Related Issues**: If your dog's behavior has suddenly changed and you suspect it may be related to a health issue, it's always best to consult with your veterinarian. Health problems can sometimes manifest as behavior changes, and it's important to rule out any underlying medical conditions.

Dealing with unwanted behaviors in your Cavalier King Charles Spaniel requires patience, understanding, and a commitment to consistent training. By identifying the root cause of the behavior, using positive reinforcement techniques, and providing adequate stimulation, most behavioral issues can be addressed successfully. However, if the behavior persists or is severe, seeking professional help can be the best course of action. With time, training, and dedication, you can correct unwanted behaviors and enjoy a happy, well-behaved dog who is a joy to live with.

CHAPTER 16

Caring for Your Senior Cavalier King Charles Spaniel

As your Cavalier King Charles Spaniel ages, their needs and care requirements will inevitably change. This chapter is dedicated to helping you navigate the challenges and rewards of caring for a senior Cavalier, from recognizing common age-related ailments to understanding when it's time to say goodbye. Senior dogs can live long, happy, and healthy lives with the right care and attention, and this chapter will provide the insights you need to make your dog's golden years as comfortable and fulfilling as possible.

Common Old-Age Ailments

Like all dogs, Cavalier King Charles Spaniels experience physical changes as they age. These changes may lead to certain health conditions that are common in senior dogs. Some of the most common old-age ailments in Cavaliers include:

1. **Arthritis**: Cavalier King Charles Spaniels are prone to arthritis as they age, particularly in their joints. This condition can cause pain, stiffness, and difficulty moving. If you notice your senior Cavalier becoming less active, having trouble jumping on furniture, or limping after walks, arthritis may be the culprit.

2. **Dental Problems**: Just like humans, senior dogs are at risk for dental issues, including periodontal disease, gum inflammation, and tooth loss. Dental care is critical for Cavaliers, as poor oral hygiene can lead to infections and other health issues, including heart problems.

3. **Heart Disease**: Cavalier King Charles Spaniels are genetically predisposed to heart disease, particularly mitral valve disease, which is common in older dogs of the breed. Symptoms may include coughing, difficulty breathing, lethargy, and a decreased tolerance for exercise.

4. **Cognitive Dysfunction Syndrome (CDS)**: Senior dogs, including Cavaliers, can develop a condition similar to Alzheimer's disease in humans called Cognitive Dysfunction Syndrome. Symptoms of CDS include confusion, disorientation, changes in behavior (such as increased anxiety or pacing), and difficulty learning new tasks.

5. **Vision and Hearing Loss**: As dogs age, they may experience a decline in their senses, particularly vision and hearing. Cataracts, glaucoma, and retinal degeneration are all common issues that affect senior dogs. While loss of vision or hearing can be managed with adaptations in your home, it can also affect their overall quality of life.

6. **Weight Gain or Loss**: Changes in metabolism, exercise habits, and diet can cause weight gain or loss in senior dogs. Cavalier King Charles Spaniels are prone to obesity, and maintaining a healthy weight is crucial to their health, especially as they age. Weight loss could also indicate underlying health issues such as cancer, kidney disease, or thyroid problems.

7. **Kidney Disease**: Older dogs are at greater risk for kidney disease, which can lead to symptoms like increased thirst, frequent urination, weight loss, and lethargy. Kidney disease can be managed with diet changes, medications, and close monitoring by a veterinarian.

8. **Incontinence**: As dogs age, they may lose control over their bladder or bowels. Incontinence can be a frustrating problem for both you and your dog, but it is manageable with the right care. Senior dogs with incontinence may require more frequent bathroom breaks, and

sometimes medications or pads can help manage the condition.

Basic Senior Dog Care

Caring for a senior Cavalier King Charles Spaniel requires some adjustments to their routine, environment, and lifestyle to accommodate their aging bodies and changing needs. While the specifics will depend on the individual dog, here are some general tips for providing excellent care for your senior dog:

1. **Adjust Exercise**: Senior dogs still need regular exercise to keep their muscles and joints strong, but the intensity and duration of their activities should be modified. Shorter walks, gentle play, and low-impact activities are ideal for senior Cavaliers. Always monitor your dog for signs of fatigue or discomfort and adjust their exercise routine accordingly.

2. **Provide a Comfortable Resting Place**: Senior dogs may experience joint pain, so providing a comfortable, supportive bed is essential. Orthopedic dog beds are ideal for older dogs, as they provide extra support and relieve pressure on aching joints. Make sure the bed is located in a quiet, easily accessible area where your dog can rest undisturbed.

3. **Monitor Weight**: Maintaining a healthy weight is crucial for senior dogs. Obesity can exacerbate joint pain, heart disease, and other health issues. On the other hand, unintentional weight loss can indicate underlying health problems. Regularly check your dog's weight and adjust their food intake and exercise accordingly.

4. **Provide Frequent Vet Visits**: Senior dogs require more frequent veterinary check-ups to monitor their health. Twice-a-year vet visits are recommended for older dogs to catch any potential issues early. Your vet may perform blood work, urine tests, and physical exams to ensure your dog's overall health is on track.

5. **Maintain Mental Stimulation**: Cognitive decline can be a concern for senior dogs, but you can help slow down the progression of Cognitive Dysfunction Syndrome (CDS) by providing mental stimulation. Use puzzle toys, interactive games, and training sessions to keep your dog's mind sharp.

6. **Modify Their Diet**: As your dog ages, their dietary needs may change. Senior dogs often benefit from food that is specifically formulated for their age group, which typically includes fewer calories, higher fiber, and added nutrients for joint health, digestive health, and cognitive

function. Speak with your vet about the best diet for your senior Cavalier.

7. **Groom Regularly**: Regular grooming is important for all dogs, but especially for senior Cavaliers. Their coats may become thinner or require more care as they age. In addition to brushing, make sure to regularly check their ears, eyes, and teeth for any signs of infection or irritation.

Illness and Injury Prevention

Preventing illness and injury in senior dogs can improve their quality of life and keep them healthy for longer. While you can't prevent every health issue, there are steps you can take to reduce the risk:

1. **Avoid Sudden Jumps or Falls**: Senior dogs with arthritis or joint problems are more vulnerable to injuries from falls or sudden movements. Help your Cavalier avoid jumping on or off furniture by providing ramps or steps to make it easier for them to get in and out of cars or onto couches and beds.

2. **Protect from Extreme Weather**: Senior dogs are more susceptible to temperature extremes. During the winter, ensure they are kept warm with appropriate bedding and coats. In the summer, be mindful of heat exhaustion and

ensure your dog has access to plenty of fresh water and shade during hot days.

3. **Prevent Infections**: Senior dogs with weakened immune systems may be more susceptible to infections. Keep an eye out for any signs of infection, including changes in appetite, lethargy, or abnormal discharge from the eyes or ears. Regular vet check-ups are essential for catching infections early.

4. **Maintain a Clean Environment**: Keeping your dog's living environment clean and free of hazards will help prevent injuries or infections. Make sure your dog's bedding is regularly cleaned, their toys are sanitized, and any potential hazards (like toxic plants or chemicals) are removed from your home.

Supplements and Nutrition

As your Cavalier ages, supplements and changes in their diet can help support their joints, heart, and overall well-being. Some common supplements for senior dogs include:

1. **Joint Supplements**: Glucosamine, chondroitin, and omega-3 fatty acids can help support joint health and reduce inflammation associated with arthritis. Talk to your vet about the right type and dosage of supplements for your dog.

2. **Antioxidants**: Antioxidants like vitamin E and vitamin C can help combat oxidative stress and support cognitive health in senior dogs. These supplements may help delay the onset of cognitive dysfunction.
3. **Probiotics**: Senior dogs often experience digestive issues. Probiotics can help promote a healthy gut microbiome and improve digestion.
4. **Omega-3 Fatty Acids**: These healthy fats support heart health and reduce inflammation. Adding fish oil or other omega-3 supplements to your dog's diet can help reduce the symptoms of arthritis and improve coat health.

Always consult your vet before starting any new supplements, as some may interact with existing medications or medical conditions.

When It's Time to Say Goodbye

One of the hardest aspects of caring for a senior Cavalier King Charles Spaniel is knowing when it's time to say goodbye. Making the decision to euthanize a beloved pet is never easy, but it's often the most compassionate choice when a dog is suffering and no longer has a good quality of life. Here are some signs that it may be time to consider this difficult decision:

1. **Chronic Pain**: If your dog is in constant pain that cannot be alleviated with medication or other treatments, and this pain is affecting their quality of life, it may be time to consider euthanasia.
2. **Loss of Mobility**: If your dog is no longer able to move around or is suffering from severe arthritis or injury that severely impacts their ability to live comfortably, it might be time to consider their overall well-being.
3. **Loss of Appetite or Inability to Eat**: If your dog is no longer eating or drinking, or if they are losing significant weight and not responding to treatment, this could indicate that their body is shutting down.
4. **Incontinence and Loss of Control**: Severe incontinence or a complete inability to control bodily functions can be a sign that the dog's body is no longer functioning as it should, especially if it's causing them significant distress.
5. **Severe Cognitive Dysfunction**: If your dog is showing signs of extreme cognitive decline, such as disorientation, pacing, or a lack of recognition, and this is severely affecting their quality of life, euthanasia may be a consideration.

The Euthanasia Process

When the time comes to say goodbye, it's important to understand the euthanasia process. While it is a heartbreaking decision, it can also be the kindest act you can do for your senior dog. Euthanasia is typically performed by a veterinarian, and it involves administering a painless injection that puts the dog to sleep. The process is quick, peaceful, and painless.

Before making the decision, spend time with your dog, ensuring that they are comfortable and loved. You can choose to be with them during the process or, in some cases, opt for a home euthanasia service that allows you to say goodbye in a familiar, peaceful setting.

Caring for a senior Cavalier King Charles Spaniel can be both rewarding and challenging. By being aware of common age-related ailments and making adjustments to their routine, diet, and environment, you can help ensure that their senior years are comfortable and fulfilling. While the eventual loss of a pet is inevitable, the memories of the love and companionship shared will last forever.

Made in United States
Cleveland, OH
21 March 2025

15372552R00089